9000972474

D1230907

101

Cheerleading Facts, Tips, and Drills

Tinker D. Murray
Mike Sardo
Gladys Keeton

COACHES
CHOICE™

ISBN-13: 978-1-58518-003-5
ISBN-10: 1-58518-003-3
Library of Congress Control Number: 2006937270
Cover design: Studio J Art & Design
Book layout: Studio J Art & Design
Front cover photo: Courtesy of Texas State University

Coaches Choice
P.O. Box 1828
Monterey, CA 93942
www.coacheschoice.com

Dedication

Thanks to our families and loved ones who have supported us in our careers and encouraged us to educate others.

Acknowledgments

The authors would like to thank the following individuals for their help in completing this project:

- Andrew Traeger (photos)
- Mrs. Mary Sardo and Zach Murray (diagrams)
- Julie Dzlema, Haley Graves, Rick Gutierrez, Kendall Jones, Caitlyn Moore, David Kyle Rowlett, Madison Wright, and Mike Sardo (photo models)
- Jim Peterson and the staff at Coaches Choice

And special thanks to the Texas State University cheerleading program (2000, 2003, and 2006 UCA All-Girl National Champions), the Texas State athletic department, and the Texas State media relations and publications department, which provided the cover photo, for allowing us to promote the quality things that they do for the university and their community.

Contents

    #1: What Do You Know About Cheerleading?
    #2: Types of Cheerleading and Participants
    #3: What Are Your Current Attitudes and Beliefs About Cheerleading?
    #4: What Is the History and Future of Cheerleading?
    #5: What Talents and Skills Do You Need to Develop to be
         Successful at Cheering?
    #6: Cheerleading Terminology
    #7: Goal Setting for Cheerleading
    #8: Are You Coachable?
    #9: Cheerleading/Spirit Internet Websites
    #10: Your Cheer Journal

    #11: Safety First
    #12: Common Cheer Injuries and Risks
    #13: Preventing Cheer Injuries
    #14: Basic Spotting Techniques
    #15: First Aid for Simple Cheer Injuries
    #16: Preventing Heat Injuries
    #17: Other Cheer Safety Challenges
    #18: Proper Cheer Equipment
    #19: Choosing a Cheer Program/Gym

Preface

This book has been developed by the authors to help beginning, intermediate, and advanced cheerleaders ages 12 through 18 improve their competitive cheerleading abilities. It is also designed to educate cheer parents, coaches, and caregivers who support cheer activities.

The tips and skills are provided to you, the reader, with the hope that you will use the right type of safety equipment (gym mats, etc.), proper coaching, and spotting (person or persons who offer assistance for your safety during a stunt or cheer move) to help you be safe and successful. Of course, you should always have fun in cheerleading activities, but the *most* important aspect of your participation in cheerleading is safety for you and your teammates.

The winning tips and drills contained in this book are based on the best scientific information currently available from the fields of cheerleading, dance, gymnastics, exercise physiology, and other sport sciences. However, you should always consult with their physician, parents, and coaches before participating in the tips and drills provided.

Remember, winning cheerleading requires that you train hard, train smart, eat healthy, and avoid risky behaviors. We hope our winning tips and drills will help you with your cheer success now and for the future.

Warning

All cheerleading activities involving movement have a potential for harm and may result in a serious injury leading to disability or death. No activities suggested or implied in this book should be attempted by individuals without their first receiving a physical examination and talking to their physician about the appropriateness of the activities for them. No activities suggested or implied in this book should be attempted by anyone without their first getting the permission of their parent or guardian. All cheerleaders should always be under the supervision of their parent or guardian, or a safety-certified cheerleading/gymnastics coach, while participating in cheerleading or gymnastics activities. All cheerleaders—regardless of age or experience—should remember that movement, involving rotation of the body, is inherently dangerous and may lead to injuries causing permanent disability or death.

No one should ever use gymnastics or cheerleading equipment (including any equipment described in this book) without having it inspected by their parent or guardian, or a safety-certified cheerleading or gymnastics coach. Inspections of equipment should take place daily, if not more frequently. Individuals should always read and understand warning labels provided by the manufacturer of any equipment they might use. In addition, they should make sure that all equipment has been properly inspected and maintained, according to the manufacturer's specifications.

No one should ever attempt cheerleading or gymnastics skills without physical assistance from a safety-certified cheerleading or gymnastics coach until the cheerleading or gymnastics coach has informed both them and their parent that they are capable of performing the skill without assistance. Attempting to perform skills without professional help before an individual is sufficiently skilled may lead to injuries causing permanent disability or death. While the use of safety equipment—including mats and padding—may reduce the potential for serious injury or death, it never eliminates that possibility. Furthermore, safety equipment never makes reckless behavior safe.

All individuals should keep in mind that they are responsible for their safety. As such, they should *never* attempt any activity if they lack appropriate training and confidence in their ability to safely perform that activity.

1

Overview and Introduction

Ronald Martinez/Getty Images

#1: What Do You Know About Cheerleading?

Objective: To determine what you know about cheerleading

Equipment Needed: Pen, paper (or computer), and your cheer journal (see Tip #10: Your Cheer Journal)

Description: The following statements are designed to help you evaluate your current knowledge about cheerleading and how to improve your cheerleading performance. Take a couple of minutes to answer these questions and determine how much cheerleading knowledge you have. Note how you did in your cheer journal. By the time you finish this book, you will not only be able to answer these questions, but many more about winning tips and skills for cheerleading. Use #8: Are You Coachable? to quickly learn more about cheerleading.

1. Cheerleading is a recognized sport like football, basketball, and volleyball. True or false?

2. Which of the following are important skills needed for success in cheerleading?
   A. Balance   C. Agility   E. All of the above
   B. Speed   D. Muscular strength

3. Cheerleading is more dangerous in terms of the number of injuries per participant than football or basketball. True or false?

4. The single most important aspect of your participation in cheerleading should be focused on _____.
   A. Safety   C. Winning   E. None of the above
   B. Having fun   D. Gaining popularity

5. Which of the following is not a sign of overtraining (doing too much too soon)?
   A. Lower resting heart rate
   B. Frequent fatigue
   C. Constant muscle soreness
   D. Insomnia (trouble sleeping)
   E. Mental burnout

6. What is the name of the stunt (see illustration) that requires you to hold your ankle and pull it up behind your head?

   A. Straddle jump
   B. Liberty
   C. Pyramid
   D. Deer
   E. None of the above

7. What is the name of the eating disorder where you don't like the way you look in terms of your body weight and you do not eat enough calories to maintain good health (you're too thin)?
   A. Bulimia
   B. Type II diabetes
   C. Anorexia nervosa
   D. Heart disease
   E. Hypertension
   (high blood pressure)

8. Females who lift weights will develop big, bulky muscles like those of males. True or false?

9. If you start lifting weights, you will be your strongest in terms of muscular strength by age 18. True or false?

10. The most important part of your cheerleading team is your coach. True or false?

Answers:

1. True and False. Cheerleading is currently recognized as an "athletic activity" by schools instead of a sport, but in club competitions it is recognized as a sport.
2. E. All of these skills and more are important to successful cheerleading.
3. False. Cheerleading has fewer injuries than football or basketball, but some cheer injuries take longer to recover from, which causes a longer loss of time from participation.
4. A. Safety is the most important aspect of your participation in cheerleading
5. A. Your resting heart rate becomes elevated by as much as 10 beats per minute or so when you are overtrained.
6. E. This stunt is called a scorpion.
7. C. Anorexia nervosa is the eating disorder where an individual does not eat enough calories to maintain her normal weight (she is too thin), which is unhealthy and leads to poor performance.
8. False. Females can get strong and increase their muscular endurance, but they do not have as much testosterone (a muscle-building hormone) as males and therefore will not get as large in terms of muscle size.
9. False. Strength gains probably peak in most males and females between 30 and 40 years of age if they continue to train as they age. You can maintain your strength and muscular endurance well into old age if you stay physically active versus becoming inactive after your competitive cheerleading days.
10. False. The most important part of your cheerleading team is you, and participating in a safe and fun environment with your teammates, coach, parents, and friends.

#2: Types of Cheerleading and Participants

Objective: To help determine which type of cheerleading is right for you

Equipment Needed: Cheer journal (see Tip #10: Your Cheer Journal)

Description: Generally speaking, you can participate in two types of cheerleading. The first type is "game" or "on the field" cheering that is usually associated with school sponsorship. A second type is "club," "competitive," or "all-star" cheering that is usually associated with a community private club or gym, and is not school-related.

Cheerleading requires large time commitments for proper conditioning, preparation, and competition. You will learn how to determine if you are ready to participate in cheerleading as well as the basics of how to prepare to compete later in the book.

Cheerleaders have opportunities to compete at the state, regional, national and international levels. In order to learn more about which type of cheerleading (perhaps both) is best for you to try and prepare for, you can you use the following tips:

- Complete Tip #8: Are You Coachable?
- Visit with your school cheer team sponsors or team members to get their advice about possible good programs in your area that you could join.
- Talk to your friends to see if they know about good club programs in your area that you could join.
- Log in your thoughts in your cheer journal about what type of cheerleader you are or want to be.

#3: What Are Your Current Attitudes and Beliefs About Cheerleading?

Objective: To learn what your current attitudes and beliefs are

Equipment Needed: Notepad, pen (or computer), and cheer journal (see Tip #10: Your Cheer Journal)

Description: At this time, it is probably important to ask yourself why you want to begin or continue to compete in cheerleading. The following list includes positive and healthy reasons to compete as a cheerleader:

- Have fun and compete in safe settings.
- Have an opportunity to be with friends and meet new friends.
- Have an opportunity to travel and compete.
- Develop and maintain your health and fitness levels.
- Develop and maintain your cheerleading skills.
- Develop your self-esteem, networking, and social skills.
- Enhance your student academic performance, as well as the rate at which you learn physical skills.
- Learn to deal positively with competitive stress.
- Develop your own level of mental toughness.

If you do not have positive reasons that motivate you to compete in cheerleading, you may want to talk with your parents, coaches, and friends about whether cheerleading is the sport for you at this time. Remember, if you decide to become a cheerleader, give yourself, your coach, and your teammates a fair amount of time to be successful. This usually takes at least six to eight weeks. If cheerleading does not end up being the activity for you, you'll still benefit by participating—even if it's only for a few weeks.

Many people believe that cheerleading is really not athletic and just depends on your popularity with schoolmates, or with parents, coaches, and cheer club members in your community. Some people also think that cheerleading is only for girls and not boys. However, in the last 20 years, cheerleading has become recognized as a "athletic activity" (not necessarily a sport) that requires the strength, speed, agility, and balance required to compete in many popular sports like football, basketball, volleyball, and gymnastics. In fact, many young girls and boys have been attracted to cheerleading because it is athletically challenging. President George W. Bush, for example, was involved in cheering at Yale University when he was in college.

At this time, you should develop your positive attitudes and beliefs about cheerleading, and learn about how you can have fun and success with your participation. You should also try to educate others around you about the positive aspects of cheerleading.

Make a list of the reasons you want to become a cheerleader or continue to participate in cheerleading, and enter them in your cheer journal. Once you have your list, evaluate it to determine if it contains mainly positive and healthy reasons. If it does not, you may want to re-evaluate your attitudes and beliefs about cheerleading.

#4: What Is the History and Future of Cheerleading?

Objective: To learn about the history and future of cheerleading

Equipment Needed: Notepad, pen (or computer), and cheer journal (see Tip #10: Your Cheer Journal)

Description: Cheerleading has been around since ancient times, when spectators cheered for competitors in the Olympic Games in Greece. The following list of events in time highlights the history of cheerleading in the U.S.:

- 1870s: The first recorded cheer was developed by male Princeton students and team supporters at the first intercollegiate football game with Rutgers.
- 1880s: The first official cheerleader at the University of Minnesota is elected "yell leader," and leads his fellow fans in cheers at games.
- 1920s: The Roaring '20s see cheerleaders (mostly men) donning school colors and using megaphones to lead cheers.
- 1940s: Lawrence Herkimer, a former gymnast and cheerleader, conducts the first workshops to train cheerleaders, and the National Cheerleaders Association (NCA) is founded. He also developed the now famous "Herkie jump" stunt.
- 1950s: The majority of cheerleaders are now female, and cheerleading is common at halftime activities at colleges and universities. Herkimer and the NCA develop the pom-pom, which is one item universally associated with cheerleading.
- 1960s: George W. Bush (the 43rd President of the United States) performs as a yell leader at Yale during his college years.
- 1970s: The NCA trains over 100,000 cheerleaders each summer at cheer camps across the country. NCA develops the first safety guidelines for cheerleaders.
- 1980s: Cheerleading receives national television exposure and the popularity of cheerleading spreads worldwide. National championships and competitive cheerleading events grow in popularity, and numerous cheerleading associations are founded.
- 1990s: Over 80 percent of the more than 3 million youth, high school, and college cheerleaders in the U.S. have a B or better grade-point average. The American Association of Cheerleading Coaches and Advisors (AACCA) is founded, and they develop safety manuals for cheering.
- 2000s: Cheerleading continues to grow at all levels, and numerous national championships are conducted throughout the U.S. School cheerleading, although not recognized as a true sport, is labeled as an "athletic activity" by the AACCA, and participants are recognized as student athletes—with many receiving at least partial scholarships to attend colleges and universities. Cheerleading is recognized as sport by many organizations because the primary purpose in club cheerleading is

competition. Cheerleading has also become part of what has been termed the "spirit industry." All National Football League (NFL) teams and a growing number of National Basketball Association (NBA) teams have cheer squads help market and promote positive images for local communities. Recently, NBA teams have added collegiate-level coed cheerleaders or stunt squads to their existing pom- and dance-style cheer groups. Business and industry are recruiting former cheerleaders to help market and promote their products to consumers. Advocates are promoting cheerleading as an Olympic demonstration competition.

Where do you think the future of cheerleading is headed? How do you think your participation in cheerleading will positively help you in your future? Write down your thoughts and enter them in your cheer journal and save them to see if you were accurate.

#5: What Talents and Skills Do You Need to Develop to be Successful at Cheering?

Objective: To identify your strengths and weaknesses, and to determine what talents and skills you need to develop to be successful in cheerleading

Equipment Needed: Notepad, pen (or computer), and cheer journal (see Tip #10: Your Cheer Journal)

Description: The talents and skills that are defined in the following section are important for you to understand in order to be better able to improve your skills in the ways discussed later in the book. You should learn the terms for the cheer-related talents and skills, and understand what they mean so that you can begin thinking about the tools you will need to try out for, make, and remain on a competitive cheerleading team. Read each term, and determine if you have the talent or skill required by taking notes in your cheer journal. Then, determine the talents and skills (your strengths and weaknesses) that you need to keep working on to develop higher levels of cheer success. The applicable terms include the following:

Aerobic fitness (or cardiovascular fitness): Activities that are rhythmic and continuous, that use large muscle groups, and that are longer in duration—like 20 to 30 minutes, for example (average levels important to maintain for cheering)

Anaerobic fitness: Activities that require quick, short bursts of energy, like sprints or tumbling skills that last 10 seconds to three minutes, for example (high ability levels required for cheering)

Agility: The ability to start, stop, and move the body quickly and in different directions (high ability levels required for cheering)

Adherence: The ability to stick with your program and a plan of action to develop your success (high ability levels required for cheering)

Balance: The ability to maintain a certain posture or to move without falling (high ability levels required for cheering)

Body composition: The amount of your body that is muscle, bone, connective tissue, and fat (average ability levels for your age and body type required for cheering)

Coachable: The ability to observe, listen, learn, practice, perform, follow rules, and work as part of a team (high ability levels are helpful for cheering)

Confidence: The ability to learn to believe in yourself and your ability to perform, as well as the ability to believe in your teammates and their ability to perform successfully (high ability levels required for cheering)

Coordination: The ability to do a task combining movements of the body and different parts of the body (high ability levels required for cheering)

Core stability: The stretching and strengthening of muscles around the spine and pelvic (trunk) muscles (high ability levels required for cheering)

Choreography: The ability to design/create dance, tumbling, and athletic movement (average to high ability levels required for cheering)

Dance: The ability to move with coordinated movements in rhythm generally to music (average to high ability levels required for cheering)

Flexibility: The ability to move a joint through the full range of motion without pain or discomfort (high ability levels required for cheering)

Mental focus: The ability to be mentally tough and understand and perform the mental aspects of cheerleading (high ability levels required for cheering)

Muscular endurance: The ability of your muscles to perform repeated contractions over a prolonged period of time (high ability levels required for cheering)

Muscular strength: The ability of your muscles to generate maximum force (high ability levels based on your age and body type required for cheering).

MVPA: Moderate-to-vigorous physical activity (high levels required for cheering)

Plyometric: Quick muscular movements like bounding or jumping up or down (high ability levels required for cheering)

Power: The ability to develop muscular strength quickly (high ability levels required for cheering)

Realistic goal setting: Involves the ability to understand that your physical and mental abilities in cheerleading will change via stages in your training, maturing rate, and your own rate of improvement rate (high ability levels required for cheering)

Reaction time: The ability to react or respond quickly to what you hear, see, or feel (high ability levels required for cheering)

Safety: The ability to avoid risky behaviors or to minimize the risk of injury when performing challenging cheer moves (high ability levels required for cheering)

Speed: The ability to move your whole body quickly forward, backward, or laterally (average to high ability levels required for cheering)

Teamwork: The ability to be coachable and work with your teammates to achieve success (high ability levels required for cheering)

Tumbling: The ability to perform gymnastics-like stunts, for example, flips and cartwheels/walkovers (average-to-high ability levels required for cheering)

Willpower: The ability to have self-discipline and practice positive cheerleading behaviors without constant supervision from coaches, parents, or peers (high ability levels required for cheering)

#6: Cheerleading Terminology

Objective: To understand some of the basic terminology used in competitive cheerleading

Equipment Needed: Notepad, pen (or computer), and cheer journal (see Tip #10: Your Cheer Journal)

Description: The terms that are defined in the following section are important for you to understand for improving your skills in the ways discussed later in the book. Read each term and determine by taking notes in your cheer journal if you understand the term, or if you need to learn more about the concept via the Internet or coaches and parents. Among the basic terminology are the following:

Base: The person in a cheer stunt who is in contact with the floor, and who lifts, supports, or elevates a cheerleader (a flyer) into the air

Basket toss: The toss of a cheerleader (a flyer) into the air, involving three to four cheerleaders. The tossing cheerleaders interlock their hands in this movement.

Chant: A short repetitive melody or yell

Cheer: A yell of applause or encouragement that usually includes body motions, mounts, and/or stunts

Cradle: The conclusion of a stunt where two or more bases—and sometimes, depending on the stunt performed, a separate head, neck, and shoulder spotter—catches a cheerleader (usually a flyer) after a toss into the air

Dismount: A way to return a cheerleader (a flyer) safely to the floor at the end of a stunt

Flyer: The cheerleader who is elevated into the air by her bases to perform a mount or stunt

Jump: Movement where both of your feet leave the ground, usually while doing a coordinated movement with your arms and legs while in the air. Examples of jumps are toe touches and hurdlers.

Liberty: A stunt where a base holds one foot of the flyer, and the flyer performs a leg motion, such as stretching the leg upward towards her head. Liberty movements include the arabesque, the scorpion, the torch, and the scale.

Motions: A set of cheerleader arm movements, such as making a "V" or the signal for a touchdown in football

Mount: Skills where one or more cheerleaders are supported in the air (also called a stunt)

Pom-pom: A fluffy ball of plastic strips connected with a handle. Used in cheering and motions by cheerleaders.

Pyramid: Multiple mounts or stunts connected together

Spotter: A cheerleader or person who is in direct contact with the floor or mat, and who is responsible for watching the person supported in the air during a stunt. The spotter is also responsible for helping catch the flyer if she should fall.

Stunt: Any movement—like a tumbling skill, toss, mount, or pyramid—usually not involving a jump

Toss: A throwing motion by bases to increase the height of a flyer so that she can become free of contact with the bases

Tumbling: A gymnastic skill, such as forward or backward rolls or walkovers, flip flops, and back tucks

Vault: A movement or stunt in which the hands of the top person are used to assist in clearing bases or props

#7: Goal Setting for Cheerleading

Objective: To help you focus and aim for success in your cheerleading experiences

Equipment Needed: Notepad, pen (or computer), and cheer journal (see Tip #10: Your Cheer Journal)

Description: Your cheerleading goals will change over time as you get better. Goals can be broken into short-term and long-term goals. For example, a short-term goal might be learning to do a front walkover tumbling skill, while a long-term goal would be making the high school varsity cheer team. It is always good to set your goals before you start a program, and to review them every two to three months to see if they still make sense to you. Practice developing a cheer goal or two, and enter them in your cheer journal.

By setting goals, you can develop a plan of action that can help you improve your skills more quickly than if you don't set goals. Use the following steps to help you in goal setting:

- Focus on one or two goals.
- Think about how you can reach the goal (training more, getting good coaching, working with a friend, etc.).
- Bounce your goals off your parents, coaches, and friends to seek their help in achieving success.
- Set a reasonable amount of time to reach your goal, and be realistic and fair to yourself by not trying to do too much, too soon.
- Check to see if you're making progress towards your goal by keeping a record of your progress in your cheer journal (see Tip #10: Your Cheer Journal).
- Reward yourself once you reach your goal, and go on to another goal (for example, enjoy yourself, be satisfied that you reached your goal, and share your achievement with your parents, coaches, and friends).

You can use the STEP system to set and review your goals. STEP stands for: Stop, Think, Evaluate, and Proceed. The STEP system can help you stay motivated in cheerleading, help you understand why you act or perform the way you do, help you become a better performer, and help you make better decisions, not only in cheerleading, but in your day-to-day life. For example, if you compete in a cheerleading competition and have a bad personal performance, you could use the STEP system to help you perform better next time. You could "stop" and think about why you did poorly (didn't get enough sleep the night before, you were sick, etc.). You then could "think" about your options and how you could do better (get more sleep the night before, wait until you recover fully from illness to compete again, etc.). You could "evaluate" by practicing your options, and then you could "proceed" by figuring out how well your plan worked. STEP is a valuable way in which you and your teammates can work together to improve your cheer skills. You should utilize the STEP system with the tips in the subsequent chapters in this book to help get you ready to perform better.

Grant Halverson/Getty Images

#8: Are You Coachable?

Objective: To help you determine if you are a coachable cheerleader

Equipment Needed: Notepad, pen (or computer), and cheer journal (see Tip #10: Your Cheer Journal)

Description: An additional cheerleading skill that is important for to have, or for you to develop for success, is the ability to be coachable (observe, listen, learn, practice, perform, and work as part of a team). To determine if you are coachable, you should be able to answer the following questions affirmatively. Make a record of your responses to the following questions about your coachability, and enter your responses in your cheer journal:

- Are you ready to be coachable?
- Are you willing to work with your current coach or instructor?
- Can you receive and follow directions easily?
- Are you ready to perform?
- Can you work with other cheerleaders as part of a team to perform (practice and condition in the off-season)?
- Are you becoming or staying engaged in the cheerleading culture? In other words, are you learning about the areas of cheerleading that will help you perform better? (Like health and fitness, nutrition, safety, injury prevention and rehabilitation, etc.)
- Are you currently engaging in regular physical activity, eating healthy, and avoiding risky behaviors?

If you answered no to more than two of these questions, you probably are not very coachable at the present time. You should probably think about ways in which you can become more coachable for your future success in cheerleading, as well as other physical activities and sports.

#9: Cheerleading/Spirit Internet Websites

Objective: To help you learn more about cheerleading via the World Wide Web by visiting some sample Internet sites

Equipment Needed: Computer and Internet access

Description: Make sure you have permission from your parent(s) or guardian before you go off web surfing these popular sites. As you probably know, some sites on the Internet are not suitable for teens to visit. So, be careful when using the Internet and when getting involved with chat-room discussions. Make sure to be safe and protect your identity and privacy when using the Internet. Also, realize that many times, the information on websites is based only on the opinions of the person(s) who developed the site, and, as a result, may not be truly accurate. Share any questions you have about a website with your parent(s), guardian, and/or coaches.

The following are some of the popular websites that promote cheerleading. This list is not meant to be inclusive. These sample websites have been chosen arbitrarily by the authors. They were all effectively in use and operative as of 7/13/06. Surf the following sites at your leisure, and of course you can always find other sites by using your Internet search engines (just surf safe).

- **About.com** www.cheerleading.about.com

  This site is a "how to" advice site with numerous cheerleading-related topics developed by individuals with high levels of knowledge and passion for the information they provide.

- **American Association of Cheerleading Coaches and Advisors** www.aacca.com

  This site is designed for cheerleading coaches and advisors and offers excellent guidelines for promoting safety for cheering.

- **American Cheer Express Corporation** (ACE) www.americancheer.com

  This site promotes cheerleading and dance with information and products that promote self-esteem, self-discipline, and good citizenship.

- **American Cheer Power** (ACP) www.cheerpower.com

  This site promotes a cheerleading and dance competition organization based in Texas that promotes cheer/dance activities in several states.

- **American Cheerleading Association** (ACA) www.acacheerleading.com

  This site promotes a cheerleading organization based in Texas, which promotes cheer camp activities in several states.

- **Cheerforce Athletic Training Center** www.cheerforce.com

  This site promotes a cheerleading gym, based in California, that has a home-page link to numerous cheerleading national and international websites.

- **Cheerleading.net** www.cheerleading.net

  This site provides extensive links to all types of cheerleading and dance on-line resources for a variety of levels, including high school, college, independents (non-school based), and international participants. It also provides numerous links to shopping opportunities for cheer/dance products.

- **National Spirit Group** (NSG) www.nationalspirit.com

  This site provides information about cheerleading and dance camps, competitions, and shopping opportunities for cheer/dance products.

- **Oak Harbor, Washington High School** (Wildcat Cheerleading)

  www.oakharborcheer.com/OHHS.html

  This site highlights the highly successful Oak Harbor High School cheerleading program, which is featured in the Coaches Choice cheerleading video/DVD series available at www.coacheschoice.com. From the home page, visit the "training corner" icon for a wealth of cheerleading information.

- **Varsity Spirit Corporation** www.varsity.com

  This site is a comprehensive link for information about cheer/dance camps, competitions, apparel, special events, and safety. It includes the Universal Cheerleaders Association (UCA), the Universal Dance Association (UDA), and the partnership of varsity and the National Federation of State High School associations (NFHS).

#10: Your Cheer Journal

Objective: To encourage you to make a journal of your cheer activities so that you can review your successes and fun times, and learn from your cheer experiences (both positive and negative)

Equipment Needed: Computer, a spiral notebook, or a three-ring binder for a hard-copy journal, or your homemade version. Optional: stickers, ribbons, pictures, drawings, or other items to decorate your journal.

Description: It is important for you to develop a personal cheer journal so that you can keep track of your progress, and you can learn to reflect on both past experiences and future circumstances about how to better prevent and treat injuries, train smarter, eat better, recover quicker, compete better, etc. Have fun with your journal, and make it something you look forward to using to record (log) the following types of information:

- Your specific goals
- The days you exercise on your own
- The days you have cheer practice
- The type of workout you do—noting the intensity, time of workout, and how you felt (hard or easy workout)
- The weather conditions (hot, cold, humid)
- Equipment that worked, or did not work
- Your feelings about how the day went, and how your workout went
- Foods and fluids that you consumed
- Any injuries that occur, or how an old injury is doing
- Weight loss or gain
- Your feelings about your progress
- The results of how you have done by performing the activities in this book
- Other items you think are important to track over time

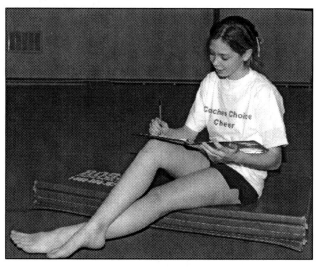

Given the aforementioned guidance about what to include in your cheer journal, design your own and start recording your cheer progress.

2

Competing and Practicing Safely

Streeter Lecka/Getty Images

#11: Safety First

Objective: To understand that the most important aspect of your participation in cheerleading is safety for you and your teammates

Equipment Needed: Pad, paper (or computer), and cheer journal

Description: It is important that you focus and develop an awareness of the need to be safe at all times when you cheer—not only yourself, but your teammates, too. You also need to make sure that you are mentally and physically ready to perform various cheer activities.

In reality, the question may be asked: how safe is cheerleading as an activity? Many people believe it is very dangerous in comparison to other sports because of the various gymnastic-like stunts that they have seen performed by cheerleaders. However, researchers have found that cheerleading carries a relatively low risk of injury. On the other hand, the injuries that do occur can occasionally be relatively serious. In fact, the number of catastrophic injuries (death and disability) in cheerleading has increased in the past decade (probably due to more gymnastic-type movements and stunts being performed). Such incidences account for half of all catastrophic injuries for females. On the other hand, the number of individuals who participate in cheerleading has increased dramatically, as well. Fortunately, most catastrophic injuries can be prevented with proper spotting and safety supervision.

As with participation in any physical activity or sport, you should know that it is common to suffer minor injuries (in part, due to the risk of being physically active versus being inactive). However, you can learn how to prevent many types of injuries, as well as how best to treat them to recover sooner. You also can minimize your risk for serious injury by always having the right type of safety equipment (gym mats, etc.), proper coaching, shoes, clothing, and spotting (person or persons who offer assistance for your safety during a stunt or cheer move) to help you be safe and successful in your cheerleading endeavors.

As a rule, cheerleading injuries occur in cheer routines that require gymnastic elements, tumbling runs, partner stunts, pyramid formations, and dance routines. Although each of these activities present a unique injury risk for cheerleaders, cheerleading is comparatively safe. For example, for participants between the ages of 5- and-24, football, basketball, soccer, and gymnastics all have higher levels of injury rates compared to cheerleading. Remember: as with other competitive sports, in order for cheerleading to be safe, it requires proper athletic skills, quality supervision, physical conditioning, and practicing safety first.

Have fun with your cheering, but please recognize that you have a duty (obligation) to yourself, your teammates, coaches, and parents to be safe at all times. Learn to condition yourself mentally and physically to participate safely in cheering. In Chapter 2, you will learn more about common cheerleading injuries and how to treat them.

Make a list of the common injuries that cheerleaders you know have had, and enter in your cheer journal. If you don't know any cheerleaders who have suffered an injury, compile a list of the types of cheer-related injuries that commonly occur. Then see Tip #12: Common Cheer Injuries and Risks to determine how accurate you were, and enter the results in your cheer journal.

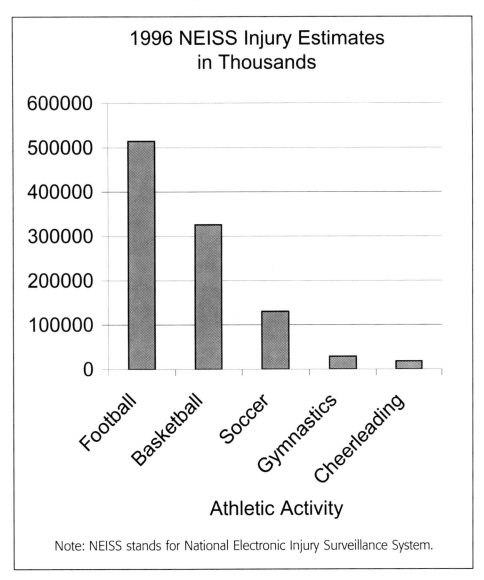

#12: Common Cheer Injuries and Risks

Objective: To understand the most common cheerleading injuries and to become aware of the risks associated with these injuries

Equipment Needed: Pad, paper (or computer), and cheer journal

Description: According to research (see chart), the most common injuries that high school and collegiate cheerleaders suffer involve the ankle, knee, hand, and back. In this regard, examples of the more common injuries are blisters, cuts, scrapes, and bruises.

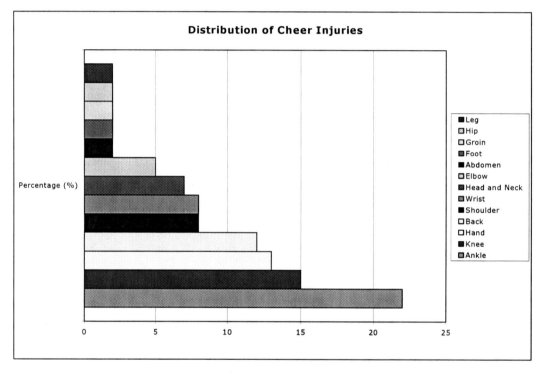

The next most common types of cheerleading injuries are ligament sprains (ligaments are bands of tissue that connect bone to bone) and muscle strains (a pull or rip in a muscle or tendon, which are bands of tissue that connect muscles to bones). Sprains involve the stretching of ligaments, and usually include local swelling of such body areas as the wrist or ankle; whereas strains involve the pulling or tearing of muscles—such as the hamstring muscle, which are the major muscles on the back of your upper thigh.

Many sprains and strains are overuse injuries that typically result from year-round cheer activity. The constant conditioning and competition associated with cheerleading may reduce the time required for full recovery from injury or the time necessary to improve an athlete's level of conditioning.

Another type of injury that sometimes occurs during cheer training and competition is an injury to the teeth or face (for example, if a flyer falls and hits a base/spotter who catches her. Heat injuries—such as heat cramps, heat exhaustion, and heat stroke—have also been reported in cheerleaders, particularly during cheer camps that are held outdoors in the summer months (see Tip #15: First Aid for Simple Cheer Injuries). In addition, cheer-related injuries, such as stress fractures (break in the bone) and lower-back pain, can result from the overuse of the limbs involved. More serious injuries to cheerleaders, such as fractures or dislocations, typically occur due to falls from stunting and poor spotting. To learn more about how to prevent catastrophic injuries (such as death or disabilities, or becoming paralyzed), consult the website of the American Association of Cheerleading Coaches and Advisors—www.aacca.com.

While not every injury can be prevented, you can reduce your risk for injuries and your ability to recover from injuries by being alert and adhering to safe practices while either training or competing. Be sure to identify, report (to sponsors, coaches, or parents), and treat injuries early. Otherwise, your injuries may get worse and increase your recovery time. Next, make a list of how you might be able to prevent common cheer injuries, and then see Tip #13: Preventing Cheer Injuries to see how accurate you were, and then enter your results in your cheer journal.

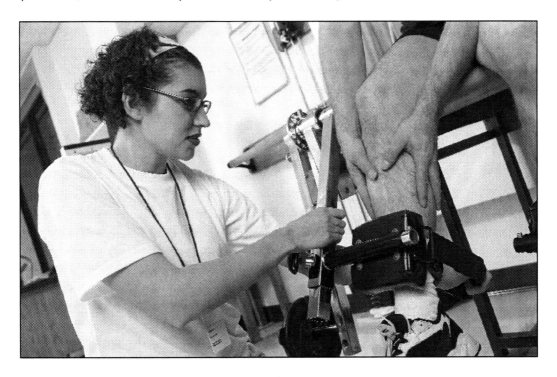

#13: Preventing Cheer Injuries

Objective: To understand how to prevent cheerleading injuries, and to become aware of how to educate others about steps that they can take to stay injury-free

Equipment Needed: Pad, paper (or computer), and cheer journal

Description: Cheerleaders often suffer injuries that are similar to those that participants in gymnastics and dance incur, since cheer movements often involve fast and explosive movements and quick stopping and then movement again. The following tips provide you with simple ways to help prevent common cheer injuries:

- Get a good pre-participation physical exam prior to beginning your cheer program (see Tip #20: Your Pre-Participation Physical Exam).
- Pay attention to your body. If you feel unusually sore or fatigued, postpone activity or exercise until you feel better.
- Practice on mats or pads that follow the standards of the American Association of Cheerleading Coaches and Advisors standards (see www.aacca.com).
- Always seek out proper medical advice when you have an injury.
- Identify, report, and treat injuries as soon as you can, before they get worse.
- Get fit to cheer, and stay fit. Do not try return to cheer activities after an injury until you have been cleared to do so medically.
- Include a proper warm-up and cool-down in your cheerleading program (see Tip #17: Other Safety Challenges).
- Monitor the frequency, intensity, time, and type (FITT) of your cheerleading exercise regimen closely. Progress slowly, but steadily.
- Wear proper shoes (see Tip #18: Proper Cheer Equipment) at all times while exercising and reflective clothing during physical activities or exercise (walking, jogging, and so on) performed in the evening when the daylight has diminished.
- Follow the cheer safety rules established by your school and/or club.
- Make sure you always have proper spotting for practice at home, school, or the cheer gym.
- Follow the emergency plan developed by the school cheer team or club.
- Learn and follow proper cheer techniques. Do not progress to difficult skills before you are ready.
- Learn to eat healthy and replace fluids lost during cheer exercise (see Chapter 5 for detailed information).
- Determine your own cheerleading physical and mental strengths and weakness and work at maintaining your strengths, while improving your weaknesses, which can help prevent injury.

At this point, review your injury prevention tip list and determine which items you are practicing and make a list of the ones on which you need improvement. Enter your responses in your cheer journal. Consult Chapter 4 for additional training tips/drills.

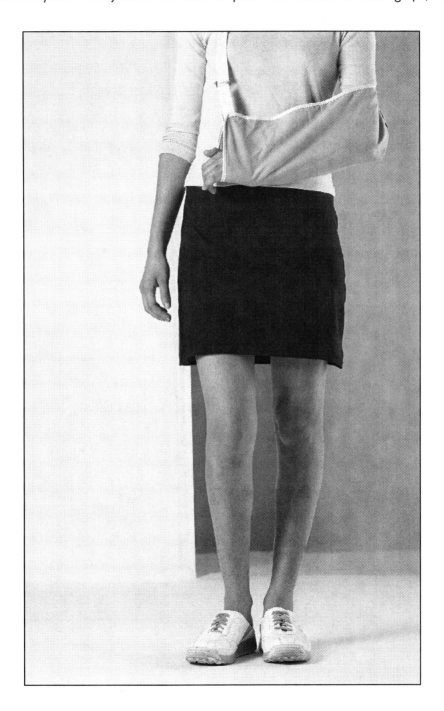

#14: Basic Spotting Techniques

Objective: To understand the basics of safe spotting and how to practice safe spotting techniques

Equipment Needed: Yourself and four cheer friends/partners

Description: Proper spotting is the most important and critical role that a cheerleader can perform as part of the cheer team. Spotting is not easy and is often taken for granted by cheerleaders. On the other hand, proper spotting can make the difference between achieving a winning performance and suffering a serious injury. Safe spotting should include at least a back spotter and a front spotter for stunts. The list on page 39 provides you with some valuable basic spotting tips. After you read the tips, practice your spotting techniques with four friends by having two of your cheer friends/partners lift the third (flyer) to their mid-thigh level on a soft surface (2-3 inch thick form mat or soft grass) and cradle her while you and the fourth person act as spotters. Rotate partners until everyone in the group feels comfortable at performing basic cheer spotting techniques. Every person involved should be completely comfortable with what they are expected to do before ever lifting a person into the air.

Basic Spotting Tips

For more advanced spotting techniques, consult your school or club sponsor or coach. Always keep in mind that you should never perform cheer stunts without adequate supervision by adults who are experienced in spotting.

- *Pay Attention*—Focus on the stunt and be prepared to catch those involved at any time without warning.
- *Reaction Time*—Practice reacting quickly and without hesitation in all cheer training and competitive situations (see Tip #28: Evaluating Your Reaction-Time Abilities).
- *Communicate*—Talk with those stunting ahead of time and have your signals worked out so that if you are the back spotter, you call out the start, break, and cradle (finish). Only one person, the back spot (or other person designated by the coach) should talk while anyone is in the air.
- *Base*—Maintain a solid base with the ground, with your feet about shoulder-width apart, and with your arms ready to catch those stunting if necessary.
- *Be Flexible*—Move with the stunt as it continues along, so that you are in close contact with those you are responsible to catch. Do not back up while stunting and get beyond reach of the flyer.
- *Be Fearless*—Remember that you are there to protect the flyer, and she should not hit the ground.
- *Know Proper Technique*—Always protect the flyer's head and neck first to minimize traumatic injury, and catch the flyer at the highest point possible.

#15: First Aid for Simple Cheer Injuries

Objective: To understand the basics of first aid for simple cheer injuries, and how to educate others about simple treatments

Equipment Needed: An elastic bandage, an ice pack, and a partner

Description: Because you should be aware of how to treat simple cheerleading injuries, you should consider taking a basic first-aid course and cardiopulmonary resuscitation (CPR) course from an agency such as the Red Cross when you have an opportunity to do so. This knowledge will help you feel more comfortable in emergency injury situations. Remember to always follow the school/club cheer emergency plan in the event of an injury (see Tip #19: Choosing a Cheer Program/Gym). Use the following guidelines to treat cheer injuries:

- *Cuts, Scrapes, and Bruises*—Because it is important to keep them clean, you should apply antiseptic medicine to them, and keep the wound covered until it is healing effectively.

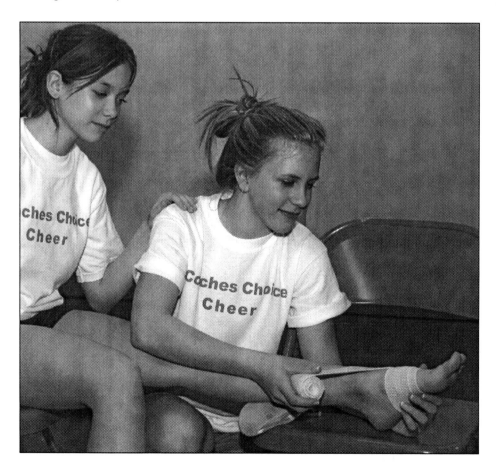

- *Blisters*—Blisters occur due to excessive friction between the skin and another surface (like your shoe). Treat a blister like a scrape or cut, and do not let it dry out. Blisters may have to be pierced with a sterile needle to release fluid that might be painful (alert your parent to this problem if it occurs).
- *Dizziness/Fainting*—Sometimes a cheerleader can get faint (i.e., light-headed) and pass out due to low blood sugar or other changes to her resting metabolism due to physical activity. If dizziness or fainting occurs, call for help, elevate the person's legs, and once she is conscious, have her drink a sip of a sports drink or orange juice.
- *Sprains, Strains, and Breaks*—It is difficult to determine the difference between these three types of injuries without having an x-ray taken. Because these injuries normally cause swelling, immediate first aid should be applied, which should adhere to the "PRICE" principle, which is an acronym derived from Protection (don't move or put pressure on the injured body part), Rest, Ice (put an ice pack or ice in a towel over the skin and injured body part), Compression (wrap an elastic bandage firmly, but not too tight, around the area), and Elevation (raise the body part to reduce the swelling).
- *Tooth Injury*—Apply pressure to any bleeding with a wet towel, or compress the area and save missing teeth in milk for possible dental repair.
- *Bloody Nose*—Apply pressure with a wet towel, or compress the area and hold the head back.
- *Head and/or Back Injury*—These injuries should always be treated as serious injuries, even if they do not turn out to be so. Do not move the person, call for help, and follow the school/club cheer emergency plan for these injuries (see Tip #17: Other Safety Challenges). Stay calm, and try to help the person remain alert and comfortable (cover with a blanket if she is cold). Do not crowd the injured person.

Having learned about how to treat cheer injuries, at this point, you should practice the "PRICE" principle. Get your elastic bandage and ice pack, practice applying the ice to the outside of your ankle with the wrap, and then elevate your ankle like it was injured. Have a partner practice on you, and then practice on her until you feel comfortable at being able to perform the necessary technique.

#16: Preventing Heat Injuries

Objective: To understand how to prevent and treat heat injuries while cheering

Equipment Needed: Pad, paper (or computer), and cheer journal

Description: Heat injuries, like heat cramps, heat exhaustion, and heat stroke, have been reported in cheerleaders—particularly during cheer camps held outdoors in the summer months. Overheating can happen because your body cannot cool fast enough by sweating when the external temperatures are high and/or the humidity is high. You can prevent heat injuries for yourself and others by paying attention to proper warning signs. After reading the following material, develop your own action plan (using the "STEP" process, see Tip #7: Goal Setting for Cheerleading) in your cheer journal to remind yourself how to avoid heat injuries.

Types of Heat Injuries

Heat Cramps—Muscle spasms resulting from large amounts of lost salt and water through sweating.

Heat Exhaustion—A serious condition that can result from excessive overheating of the body. Normal symptoms of this condition are cold, clammy skin and dizziness or shock. Other symptoms can include headache, feeling of weakness, rapid heart rate, upset stomach, and heavy sweating.

Heat Stroke—The most serious heat-related condition that results in high body temperatures (the skin is very hot). If a person suffering from a heat stroke loses consciousness, you should immediately call 911 for medical help.

Heat-Injury Treatment

Heat Cramps—Make sure you are drinking plenty of fluids, and if you sweat heavily (i.e., if you see lots of salt stains on your shirt), you may need to get more salt in your diet, which can help prevent cramping (see Tip #54: Your Cheer Iron, Calcium, and Salt Dietary Needs).

Heat Exhaustion—Stop the cheer activity, move to a shaded, cool area (helpful if it is close to a breeze or a fan), and drink fluids. It can also be helpful to lie in a wading pool (e.g., a plastic, blow-up model) that can be filled with water and placed in the shade by the cheer practice field. Do not return to practice until you have fully recovered, which usually one to two days. Prior to returning to cheer activities, you should seek medical clearance.

Heat Stroke—Seek medical help immediately, because a heat stroke can be fatal.

Heat-Injury Prevention

Get Acclimatized—Allow your body to get used to working in the heat slowly. For example, if you know you are going to summer cheer camp, start getting used to the daytime heat by working out in it for 20 minutes, and then working up to 30-to-60 minutes for 5-to-10 days ahead of the camp date.

Take in Fluids—Drink plenty of fluids before, during, and after the cheer activities.
- Before: Consume between one-and-a-half and two-and-a-half cups of cold water 10-to-20 minutes before exercising in the heat (one cup = eight ounces). Drink before you become thirsty, or you are probably already dehydrated (and at risk for heat injury).
- During: During physical activity in the heat, attempt to match fluid loss with fluid intake. A rule of thumb would be to drink approximately one cup of water every 10-to-15 minutes.
- After: Continue drinking water afterward, even if you do not feel thirsty. It may take up-to-12 hours to achieve complete fluid replacement after strenuous exercise in the heat.

For most situations, water works as well as any beverage in preventing dehydration (loss of fluids) for activities lasting up-to-30 minutes in duration. For cheer activities lasting longer than 30-to-60 minutes, you can also choose one of the many sports drinks on the market (best to choose one that has five-to-eight percent carbohydrate-sugar in it—check the product label). Avoid beverages that are carbonated and/or that contain caffeine. Such beverages are absorbed at a much slower rate than plain water, and can cause you to become dehydrated.

Clothing—Wear lightweight (cotton), loose-fitting, light-colored clothing in the heat. Wear a hat, if possible, to protect your head from the sun, and remember to wear sunscreen to prevent sunburn. Make sure the hat you wear does not obstruct your vision or fly off your head easily while tumbling or stunting. Also make sure you rub sunscreen in thoroughly so that it is not slippery when you are spotting. Be sure to choose clothing that does not interfere with the activities in which you are participating. Stunting with long sleeves can be dangerous for bases (especially if the sleeves are loose-fitting). Wearing long pants for flyers can also be dangerous while stunting.

Recovering Day-to-Day—When you have a cheer camp lasting several days in hot conditions, be sure to eat plenty of carbohydrates (see Tip #52: Your Cheer Carbohydrate Dietary Needs), and drink plenty of fluids during your off time from cheer. Weigh yourself before and after each cheer practice. You should be within one-to-two pounds of your "before" weight before you participate again in strenuous cheer activities.

#17: Other Cheer-Safety Challenges

Objective: To understand to prevent and treat other cheer-safety challenges

Equipment Needed: Pad and paper (or computer)

Description: Three other cheer-safety issues of which you should be aware are asthma, staph infections, and concussions. The material in this tip is designed to help explain these cheer-safety challenges. After reading the material, develop your own action plan (using the "STEP" process, see Tip #7: Goal Setting for Cheerleading) to remind yourself how to deal with these particular cheer-safety challenges:

Asthma

Asthma is the one of the most common reasons that cheerleaders miss or have to modify their practice time. Asthma is a disease that causes the air passages in the lungs to swell or narrow (bronchospasm), making it harder for you to breathe.

Signs and Symptoms of Asthma
• Coughing
• Wheezing (a hoarse whistling sound heard during exhalation)
• Shortness of breath
• Chest tightness

Causes or Conditions that Aggravate Asthma
• Poor medical management
• Air pollution (mold, pollens, tobacco, dust mites, etc.)
• Emotions (like laughing or crying)
• Allergies
• Exposure to cold air

Strategies to Control Asthma
• Make sure to get a medical evaluation of the problem.
• Make sure you have your personal inhaler (if prescribed by your doctor) close by, and take a backup inhaler when you travel to compete (do not use someone else's inhaler). If your asthma is under control, you should not have to use your inhaler more than twice in any one day.
• Make sure you perform a 15-minute, minimum warm-up before engaging in cheer activities.

- Make sure that you do not exercise at high intensities in cold weather until you have a proper warm-up, because doing so may make your asthma worse.

Staph

Staph (or *staphylococcus aureus*) infections are like boils, or soft-tissue infections, that can cause you serious health problems. Staph infections can occur in the armpit, groin, or genital areas, and, most frequently, the inside of the nose. They often are confused with a "spider bite"-type of infection. Most infections occur through direct physical contact of the staph bacteria with a break in the skin (cut or scrape), or during contact with objects like dirty clothing, bed linens, or towels soiled with wound drainage. Your hands must be clean before you touch your eyes, nose, mouth, or any cuts or scrapes on the skin.

Strategies to Control Staph Infections
- Perform routine (daily) skin exams.
- Report a cut or scrape that does not heal to your parents and coach/sponsor.
- Wash your hands regularly, and use alcohol hand gels when you can.
- Clean your cheer equipment regularly with chlorhexidine (Phisohex).
- Clean your clothing daily. Do not share towels or soiled clothing.
- Perform thorough hand washing after contact with any wound or cut (such as when stunting).
- Keep wounds clean, use topical antibiotics, and use bandages.
- Seek medical advice early.
- Use antibiotics as prescribed, and do not discontinue them until told to do so.

Concussions

Concussions are head injuries that can cause a cheerleader to be dazed, to feel as if she had her "bell rung," or to become unconscious. Cheerleaders can suffer concussions due to falls or collisions during stunting. To help prevent concussions, follow safe cheering recommendations. Refer to Tip #11 through Tip #14, which provide safety information.

Signs and Symptoms of Concussions
- Confusion
- Amnesia (can't remember things)
- Dazed look or vacant stare
- Slurred or incoherent speech
- Vomiting and/or nausea
- Slow movement and verbal responses
- Rapidly changing emotions
- Poor coordination
- Dizziness
- Headaches
- Restlessness

Strategies to Control Your Risk of Suffering a Concussion

- Follow all proper cheer safety rules and proper safety techniques for stunting.
- Seek medical attention, and do not return to cheer activities until cleared to do so by a physician.

#18: Proper Cheer Equipment

Objective: To become aware of how to select proper cheer equipment

Equipment Needed: Computer and Internet access

Description: Three of the main cheer-equipment factors with which you ought to become more familiar involve the selection of appropriate cheer clothing, cheer footwear, and matting or cushioning for home cheer practice. Once you have reviewed the equipment recommendations detailed in this tip, go online and search the websites listed in Tip #9 to obtain additional information on cheer clothing, cheer footwear, and cheer mats.

Cheer Clothing Considerations

- Should be comfortable (not necessarily expensive)
- Should fit well, but allow stretching as you move
- Women should buy a sports bra that is designed for cheer activities.
- Men should buy sport briefs, or an athletic supporter, for cheer activities.
- Most cheer teams have specific clothing rules, but you can often save money on cheer clothing by shopping around (either online or in person).

Cheer Footwear Considerations

- Before you buy shoes, visit a local sporting goods store and seek out the advice of a knowledgeable salesperson. You might also ask your cheer coach or sponsor for advice.
- Try on shoes before you buy them.
- Walk around in the store to make sure the shoes are comfortable. Be sure to try on shoes while wearing the same type of socks that you intend to wear during cheering.
- Be aware that cheer shoes typically cost between $40 and $100.
- Look for quality, because when it comes to shoes, be sure not to compromise on comfort and fit. A quality pair of shoes almost always lasts longer than an inexpensive brand, and will be better for your feet.
- Choose comfortable shoes over shoes that look good. If you feel you must have the latest shoe from a company with a well-known name, don't settle for a poor fit because of its look.
- Know when to replace your shoes. Knowing when to replace your shoes is as important as any other shopping consideration. Once a cheer shoe starts to lose its sole and support, it should no longer be used for cheer activities. Such a shoe could do more harm than good to your feet and joints.

- Have a spare pair of cheer shoes, if possible. You should have a second pair of fitness shoes and alternate their use. This step will give one pair at a time to dry out and regain their cushioning effect. This strategy will provide you with the support you need, and can extend the life of your shoes significantly.
- Make sure that the shoes you choose fit the skills that you need to perform when cheerleading. For example, if you tumble a lot, light shoes may be more attractive to you than heavier ones. If you are a flyer, your bases need to like the feel of your shoes in their hands.

Cheer Matting/Cushioning Considerations

- All cheer gym facilities (school or club) should provide proper mats for cheer stunting (see www.aacca.com for recommendations from the American Association of Cheerleading Coaches and Advisors).
- You can buy mats for home cheer practice from a variety of sources. Mats should be at least $1\frac{3}{8}$ inches thick, and long and wide enough to cover your practice area.
- Cheer mats for home use typically cost between $100 and $300, and can be purchased online or in person at various sporting goods or specialty stores.

Brian Bahr/Getty Images

#19: Choosing a Cheer Program/Gym

Objective: To become aware of how to select a cheer program/gym to meet your needs

Equipment Needed: Transportation, telephone, and/or computer with Internet access

Description: As you have learned, you have several options and considerations when you decide to become a cheerleader. One of those considerations is choosing a cheer program or gym to tryout for (or join). The following recommendations can help you make a more informed decision about choosing a cheer program or gym. Once you have read and reviewed the items below, travel to two or three cheer local facilities close to you (or call, or go online for information), and determine which facilities meet your individual needs and will help you have future cheer success.

Characteristics of a Quality Cheer Program/Gym

- Cheer instructors/coaches with a degree in physical education (or related area) and documented experience in cheer safety, the teaching of cheer skills (such as stunts and jumps), successful coaching experience, and a caring attitude
- Cheer instructor/coach/staff certifications in first aid, CPR, and (if available) automated external defibrillators (AEDs)
- Polices that require an annual pre-participation physical exam for all participants
- An emergency plan for the facility. You should ask for a copy of the plan. It should contain specific actions for the instructor/coach, staff, and cheer participants to follow in case of an emergency. The plan should have emergency contact numbers and should mandate that the steps of the plan be practiced regularly to ensure that everyone knows how to respond if an emergency situation should arise.
- A posted list of safety rules for spotting, for mats, for the wearing of jewelry, etc.
- A seasonal conditioning program to help cheerleaders maintain their fitness levels in the off-season, pre-season, and competitive season
- A published business plan and a list of fees for participation in day-to-day training, uniforms, and competitions
- A manual of procedures (both written and online) for day-to-day operations, such as appropriate supervision, policies for spectators, practice schedules, discipline issues, and try-outs

Observations and Questions You Should Ask to Assess the Level of Quality of a Cheer Program/Gym

- Visit with participants of the program/gym in which you are interested.

- Meet instructors/coaches and find out their expectations and cheerleading credentials.
- Inspect the facility to see if it is clean and safe.
- Attend a practice, and watch the interaction of participants and the instructor/coach.
- Attend a competition where the school or club is involved (if possible) to see how the team and coaches interact.
- Visit with friends and/or current and former team members to see what they think of their experiences with the team.

3

Getting Physically Ready to Cheer

Jamie Squire/Getty Images

#20: Your Pre-Participation Physical Exam

Objective: To become aware of the need and requirements for a pre-participation physical exam and of factors that may limit your participation in cheering

Equipment Needed: Telephone and/or computer with Internet access

Description: Before you will be allowed to cheer in a school or club setting, you will need to have a pre-participation sports examination (PSE) before the season and activity begins. The primary purpose of the PSE is to maximize safe participation for yourself. The PSE should include a sports/physical activity history and a physical examination. The components of the pre-participation sports examination should include the following:

- Completion of a comprehensive questionnaire about your health history
- Measurement of heart rate and blood pressure
- Auscultation of (listening to) your heart and lungs
- Evaluation of your extremities (arms/legs) for pulses, reflexes, and injuries
- Screening for medical problems and risks of life-threatening complications during participation

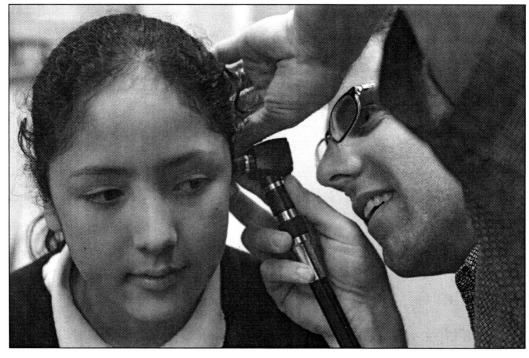

Tim Boyle/Getty Images

- Screening to identify conditions that require a treatment plan before or during participation
- Screening to identify and rehabilitate old musculoskeletal injuries
- Screening to identify and treat conditions that interfere with performance
- Screening to remove unnecessary restrictions on participation
- Screening to advise cheerleaders in regards to the most appropriate activities (for example, base versus flying) in which they should participate.

A limited number of medical conditions exist that may limit your participation in cheerleading because they are associated with life-threatening complications. However, the actual risk for sudden death in young people age 6-through-17 is only between 1-in-100,000 and 1-in-300,000 participants. The risk of sudden death is much higher in males compared with females. The reason for the higher sudden death risk in males versus females is unknown at this time.

Some cardiovascular conditions that can increase the risk of sudden death in young athletes and may limit the athlete's participation include:
- Hypertrophic cardiomyopathy—enlarged heart
- Coronary artery anomalies—abnormal coronary arteries
- Marfan syndrome—Aortic (large artery exiting heart) rupture
- Myocarditis—heart infection
- Arrhythmia—abnormal skipped beats

Having learned about the basics of a PSE, contact the cheer program/gym to which you belong to find out what its policies are for pre-physical examinations. Do this by calling or going online to determine if you will need to schedule your own appointment for an exam, or if the program/gym arranges the exams. Make sure that if you have to make the exam appointment, that you (or your parents) arrange the appointment well ahead of the start date to begin cheer practice.

#21: Evaluating Your Cheer-Fitness Levels

Objective: To learn why it is important to regularly evaluate your cheer-fitness levels, and what abilities need to be evaluated

Equipment Needed: Pad, paper (or computer), and cheer journal

Description: As you learned in Tip #5: What Talents and Skills Do You Need to Develop to be Successful at Cheering?, you need particular talents and skills to be successful in cheerleading. This Tip details 12 abilities that you should evaluate regularly to determine your strengths and weaknesses related to cheering. You should learn to test yourself on all the following talents and skills covered in Chapter 3. By learning to evaluate your strengths and weaknesses, you can focus on maintaining your strengths, while improving your weaknesses. As in Tip #5: What Talents and Skills Do You Need to Develop to be Successful at Cheering?, have a pen, pad (or computer), and your cheer journal ready to check off the following talents or skills in which you feel you are strong or weak:

Talent/Skill	Strong	Weak
Agility		
Balance		
Coordination		
Core Stability		
Speed		
Power		
Reaction Time		
Aerobic Fitness		
Muscular Strength		
Muscular Endurance		
Flexibility		
Body Composition		

#22: Evaluating Your Agility Levels

Objective: To learn how to test and evaluate your basic agility levels

Equipment Needed: A flat, non-skid surface, tape (or chalk to write on a sidewalk), a stopwatch, and a partner to time and count the number of lines crossed

Description: Use tape or chalk and mark off an area like that shown in the diagram, with each block three feet apart and three feet wide. Start by standing and straddling the center line or start. Shuffle your feet (left to right, and so on) as fast as you can to reach and straddle the outside line on the right and then back to the left. Do not cross your feet. Try to cross as many lines as you can in 10 seconds.* Your goal should be to cross 30 lines. Practice until you can demonstrate the relatively high levels of agility that you will need to perform your cheerleading routines.

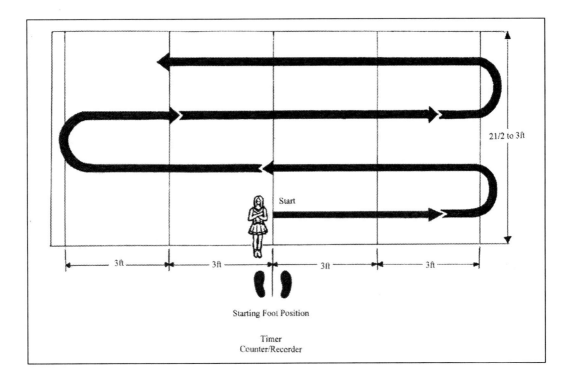

21/2 to 3ft

Start

3 ft   3 ft   3 ft   3 ft

Starting Foot Position

Timer
Counter/Recorder

*You or your coach/instructor may vary the evaluation standards to be more specific to your particular cheer needs.

#23: Evaluating Your Balance Ability

Objective: To learn how to test and evaluate your basic balance abilities

Equipment Needed: A flat, nonskid surface, a stopwatch, and a partner to time and spot

Description: For one-foot balance, begin by removing your shoes and socks. Stand on your dominant (favorite) foot, and place the other foot on the inside of your opposite leg at calf level (Figure A). Put your hands on your waist, and when your partner says, "Start," raise up on the ball of your dominant foot. Your partner should time how long you can maintain this balanced position before you have to hop, twist, or touch the floor. Your goal is to maintain the balanced position for 30 seconds or longer. Practice until you can demonstrate the relatively high levels of agility that you will need to perform your cheerleading routines.

For squat balance, begin by squatting down with your hands on the floor shoulder-width apart (a cheer mat and a spotter are recommended). Try to put your knees on your elbows so that you are balancing your body weight (Figure B)*. Your goal should be to maintain the balanced position for longer than 20 seconds. Practice until you can demonstrate the relatively high levels of agility that you will need to perform your cheerleading routines.

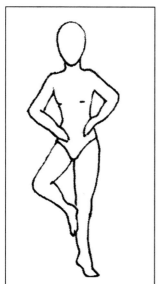

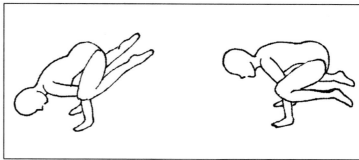

Figure A   Figure B

*You or your coach/instructor may vary the evaluation standards to be more specific to your particular cheer needs.

#24: Evaluating Your Level of Coordination

Objective: To learn how to test and evaluate your level of basic coordination

Equipment Needed: Two bandanas (or plastic shopping bags) and a partner

Description: Place the bandanas or bags in your dominant (favorite) hand as shown in the diagram. Lift your arm up, and drop one bandana or bag and repeat, quickly dropping the other bandana or bag. Catch each bandana or bag before it hits the ground, and keep the cycle going until one of the two items falls to the ground. Have your partner count the successful number of catches to determine your hand-eye coordination skill level. Your goal should be to achieve at least 12 consecutive catches. Practice until you can demonstrate the relatively high levels of coordination that you will need to perform your cheerleading routines.

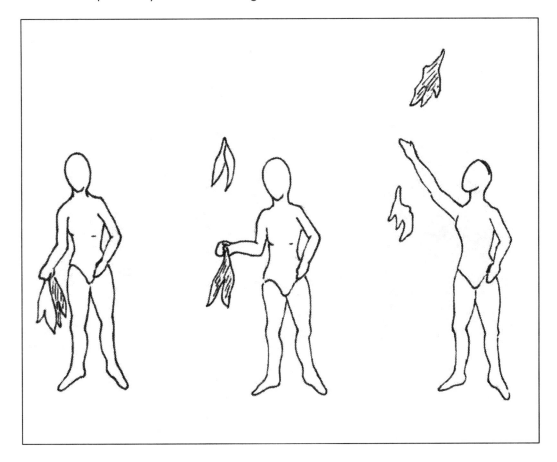

*You or your coach/instructor may vary the evaluation standards to be more specific to your particular cheer needs.

#25: Evaluating Your Level of Core Stability

Objective: To learn how to test and evaluate your basic level of core stability

Equipment Needed: A flat, nonskid surface (using a cheer mat is recommended), a partner, and a stopwatch

Description: To start, assume the push-up position as shown in the diagram. Have your partner time you as you do the following and see if you can achieve the specified goal times:

- Hold the standard push-up position with your back straight and chin at least six inches from the mat for 45 seconds. Rest for 10 seconds.
- Resume the push-up position, lift your right leg off the ground, and hold for 20 seconds. Rest for 10 seconds.
- Resume the push-up position, lift your right arm off the ground, and hold for 20 seconds. Rest for 10 seconds.
- Resume the push-up position, lift your left leg off the ground, and hold for 20 seconds. Rest for 10 seconds.
- Resume the push-up position, lift your left leg off the ground, and hold for 20 seconds. Rest for 10 seconds.
- Resume the push-up position, lift your right arm and right leg off the ground, and hold for 20 seconds. Rest for 10 seconds.
- Resume the push-up position, lift your left arm and left leg off the ground, and hold for 20 seconds. Rest for 10 seconds.
- Practice until you meet the time goals for the core stability drills that you will use in your cheerleading routines.*

*You or your coach/instructor may vary the evaluation standards to be more specific to your particular cheer needs.

#26: Evaluating Your Running Speed

Objective: To learn how to test and evaluate your running speed

Equipment Needed: A flat, nonskid surface at least 70-to-80 yards long, a stopwatch, and a partner

Description: Determine a starting line so that you can run 50 yards without stopping. After you have warmed-up properly, have your partner stand at the 50-yard marker and raise one arm. Start sprinting when your partner drops her arm and run all the way across the finish line. Rest for 5-to-10 minutes and try again. Record your two best times and determine an average of your scores.* Your goal is to run 50 yards in less than eight seconds. Practice until you can demonstrate the relatively high levels of foot speed that you will need to perform your cheerleading routines.

*You or your coach/instructor may vary the evaluation standards to be more specific to your particular cheer needs.

#27: Evaluating Your Level of Explosive Power

Objective: To learn how to test and evaluate your level of basic explosive power

Equipment Needed: A flat, nonskid surface at least 10 feet long next to a wall 10-to-12 feet or higher that you can mark on (home garage, gym, etc.), chalk to mark on the wall, a tape measure, and a partner to help with measurements

Description: To determine your vertical jump ability, start by standing with your dominant arm next to the wall, with a piece of chalk in your hand (Figure A). Start with both feet together, and place a chalk mark at the highest level you can reach with your dominant arm, while standing flatfooted (i.e., not on your toes). Take one step back after you make the mark, step forward, and jump straight up as far as possible, and make another chalk mark. Have your partner help you measure the distance between the marks in inches to get your vertical leap score. Your goal is to jump vertically 15 inches or more.* Practice until you can demonstrate the relatively high levels of leg power that you will need to perform your cheerleading routines.

   To assess your standing long jump ability, start by drawing a starting line. Stand behind the line with your feet shoulder-width apart and your toes nearly touching the line (Figure B). Bend downward, throw your arms behind your body, and then jump forward (while moving your arms forward) as far as possible (Figure C). Have your partner measure (in inches) where the back of your heels land.* Try not to fall backwards. Your goal is to jump 72 inches or further. Practice until you can demonstrate the relatively high levels of explosive power that you will need to perform your cheerleading routines.

---

*You or your coach/instructor may vary the evaluation standards to be more specific to your particular cheer needs.

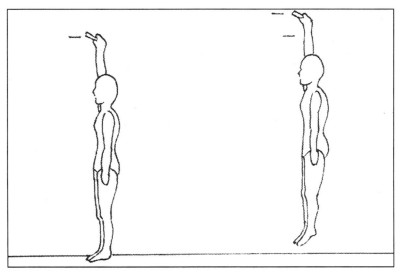

Figure A

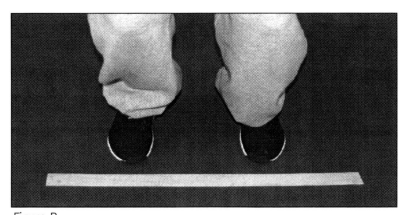

Figure B

Figure C

#28: Evaluating Your Level of Reaction Time

Objective: To learn how to test and evaluate your level of basic reaction time

Equipment Needed: A table (e.g., a dining room table or a card table), a chair, a yardstick, and a partner

Description: Start by sitting in the chair with your dominant (favorite) arm resting on the table as shown in the diagram. Extend your fingers (thumb and index finger) over the edge of the table two to three inches, spread them apart about two inches, and have your partner line up the yardstick so that the zero point is even with the top of your thumb. Have your partner drop or let go of the yardstick. Focus on the yardstick as your partner drops it, and catch it as soon as you can. Try this three times, score each try to the nearest half inch, and then determine an average of your scores. Your goal is to catch the yardstick within two inches of when it is dropped.* Practice until you can demonstrate the relatively high levels of reaction time that you will need for your cheerleading routines.

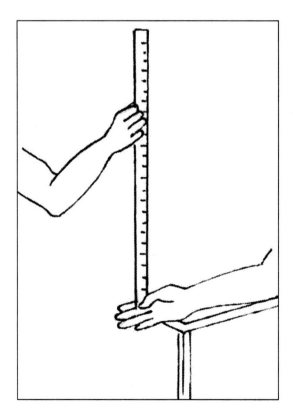

*You or your coach/instructor may vary the evaluation standards to be more specific to your particular cheer needs.

#29: Evaluating Your Aerobic-Fitness Level

Objective: To learn how to test and evaluate your basic aerobic fitness level

Equipment Needed: A flat, nonskid surface at least 200 meters long that is accurately measured, and comfortable walking/jogging shoes (see Tip #18: Proper Cheer Equipment for more information)

Description: Condition yourself by walking and jogging for six weeks or so before attempting to complete either the 20-minute steady-state jog or the 30-minute steady-state walk.

- **20-minute steady-state jog**—Once you have selected a safe jogging course, warm up, and then try to cover two miles in 20 minutes of continuous slow jogging.* Make sure you learn to pace yourself (so that you can exercise continuously for the entire time without experiencing undue stress/discomfort). Test yourself only when the weather is relatively nice (if outside: low wind, comfortable temperature). Cool down afterward. Practice until you achieve your basic goal for aerobic fitness that you will need to perform your cheerleading routines.

- **30-minute steady-state walk**—Once you have selected a safe walking course, warm up, and then try to cover 2.2 miles in 30 minutes of continuous slow walking.* Make sure you learn to pace yourself (so that you can exercise for the entire time without experiencing undue stress/discomfort). Test yourself only when the weather is relatively nice (if outside: low wind, comfortable temperature). Cool down afterward. Practice until you achieve your basic goal for aerobic fitness that you will need to perform your cheerleading routines.

*You or your coach/instructor may vary the evaluation standards to be more specific to your particular cheer needs.

#30: Evaluating Your Level of Muscular Strength

Objective: To learn how to test and evaluate your basic level of muscular strength

Equipment Needed: A flat, nonskid surface (using a cheer mat is recommended), a pull-up bar as per the diagram, a stopwatch, and a partner

Description:

- **Push-Ups**—Assume a standard push-up position (Figure A). Lower your body until your elbows are at a 90-degree angle, and then repeat at a rate of about one push-up every three seconds. Have your partner count the total number of push-ups that you can do before you have to stop (or when you can't properly perform one every three seconds). Your goal is to complete 15 push-ups.* Practice until you can achieve your basic goal for muscular fitness that will enable you to perform your cheerleading routines.
- **Pull-Ups**—Assume a hanging position on a pull-up bar (Figure B), and pull yourself up (with your chin over the bar) as many times as you can before you fatigue. Have your partner count the total number of pull-ups you can do. Your goal is to complete two to three pull-ups.* Practice until you can achieve your basic goal for muscular fitness that will enable you to perform your cheerleading routines.
- **Keep Your Chin Up**—Assume a hanging position (Figure C), and pull yourself up (with your chin over the bar), and hang in that position as long as you can, while your partner times you. Your goal is to hang for 20 seconds.* Practice until you can achieve your basic goal for muscular fitness that will enable you to perform your cheerleading routines.

---

*You or your coach/instructor may vary the evaluation standards to be more specific to your particular cheer needs.

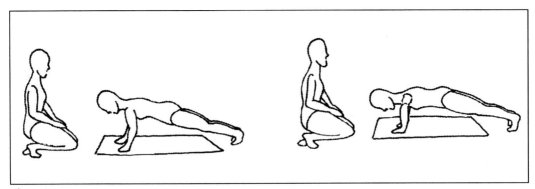

Figure A

Figure B

Figure C

#31: Evaluating Your Level of Flexibility

Objective: To learn how to test and evaluate your basic level of flexibility

Equipment Needed: A computer or pen and paper, a flexible tape measure (e.g., plastic or cloth), a box 12-inches high, two yardsticks, a tape, a cheer mat, and a partner with whom you are comfortable working and willing to share your measurements.

Description:

- **Sit and Extend**—Use a 12-inch-high box (a cardboard box will do) with a yardstick taped on top of the box so that it extends nine inches toward you. The zero end of the yardstick should be nearest you. Remove your shoes, and place your feet against the box, with your legs straight. Bend forward slowly (keeping your legs straight), and stretch as far forward as possible, with your arms moving along the yardstick. Have your partner record your best three tries (in inches), detailing how far you reached beyond the edge of the box (beyond nine inches). Your goal is to reach at least three inches past your toes (or 12 inches).* Practice until you can achieve your basic goal for flexibility that will enable you to perform your cheerleading routines.

- **Get Your Chin Up**—Lie face down on a cheer mat, with your hands under the top of your thighs (Figure A). Raise your chin as high as you can, and hold the position for two to three seconds, while keeping your legs flat on the mat (hint: you may need another partner to help hold your legs down). Have your partner record your best three tries (in inches), detailing how high your chin was above the mat. Your goal is to rise up 12 inches from the mat.* Practice until you can achieve your basic goal for muscular fitness that will enable you to perform your cheerleading routines.

- **Arm Lift**—Lie face down on a cheer mat, with your hands above your head, about shoulder-width apart (Figure B). Have your partner give you a yardstick to hold in your hands. While keeping your chin on the mat, slowly lift the yardstick up above your head as far as you can. Have your partner record your best three tries (in inches), detailing how high the yardstick was above the mat. Your goal is to rise up 12 inches from the mat.* Practice until you can achieve your basic goal for muscular fitness that will enable you to perform your cheerleading routines.

*You or your coach/instructor may vary the evaluation standards to be more specific to your particular cheer needs.

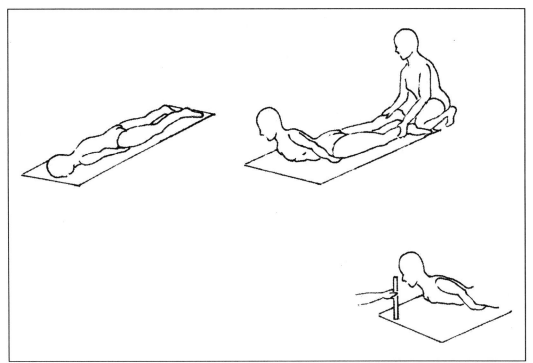

Figure A

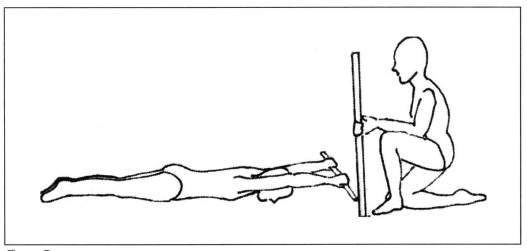

Figure B

#32: Evaluating Your Level of Body Composition

Objective: To learn how to test and evaluate your basic level of body composition

Equipment Needed: A computer, a flexible tape measure (e.g., plastic or cloth), and a partner with whom you are comfortable working and willing to share your measurements.

Description:

- **Body Mass Index (BMI)**—This measurement uses your age, height, and weight to help determine if you are underweight, overweight, or at risk of becoming overweight. To determine your BMI, go to the website for the Centers for Disease Control and Prevention (CDC), http://www.cdc.gov/nccdphp/dnpa/bmi/, and click on the link for teen BMI calculator. Follow the instructions by entering your gender, height, and weight, and your BMI will be calculated. Your BMI should be above the fifth percentile (too lean) and below the 85th-to-95th percentile (too heavy) for optimal cheerleading performance.* See Chapter 5 to learn how to control your body weight in healthy and nutritional ways.
- **Waist Circumference**—Measuring your waist circumference is a good way to determine if you are carrying too much fat around your abdomen (stomach), which may negatively influence your cheer abilities. To determine your waist girth (diameter), use a flexible tape measure to determine your waist circumference (have a partner measure your waist). Take the measurement at the level of your

*You or your coach/instructor may vary the evaluation standards to be more specific to your particular cheer needs.

umbilicus (bellybutton) in inches, and remember to put the tape snug (but not too tight). Use the following table to see if you are within the appropriate range for your age and gender. If not, you may need to gain or lose weight to improve your ability to perform cheer activities. See Chapter 5 to learn about controlling your body weight in healthy and nutritional ways.

Age	Waist Size for Girls	Waist Size for Boys
12	23–29 inches	24–29 inches
13	24–30 inches	24–30 inches
14	24–32 inches	25–31 inches
15	24–32 inches	25–31 inches
16	25–33 inches	25–32 inches
17	25–34 inches	26–33 inches
18	25–35 inches	27–34 inches

Reference: Fernandez, J.R., et al (2004). J. Pediatrics. 145: 439–444.

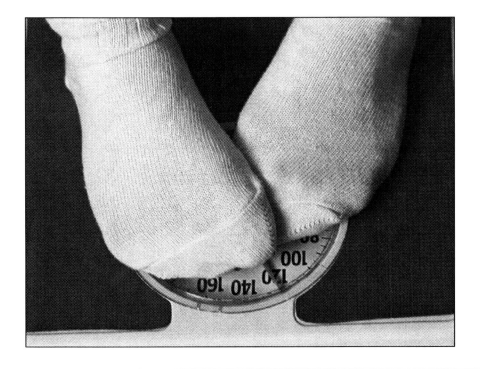

#33: Evaluating Your Level of Muscular Endurance

Objective: To learn how to test and evaluate your basic level of muscular endurance

Equipment Needed: A flat, nonskid surface (using a cheer mat is recommended), and a partner

Description:

- **Push-Ups**—Assume a standard push-up position (Figure A). Lower your body until your elbows are at a 90-degree angle, and then repeat at a rate of about one push-up every three seconds. Have your partner count the total number of push-ups that you can do before you have to stop (or when you can't perform properly one every three seconds). Your goal is to complete 15 push-ups.* Practice until you can achieve your basic goal for muscular fitness that will enable you to perform your cheerleading routines.

- **Curl-Ups**—Lie on your back on the mat, with your knees bent slightly (Figure B). Slowly raise your head and upper body until you get halfway to your bent knees. Repeat at a rate of about one curl-up every three seconds. Have your partner count the total number of curl-ups that you can do before you have to stop (or when you can't properly perform one every three seconds). Your goal is to complete 25 curl-ups.* Practice until you can achieve your basic goal for muscular fitness that will enable you to perform your cheerleading routines.

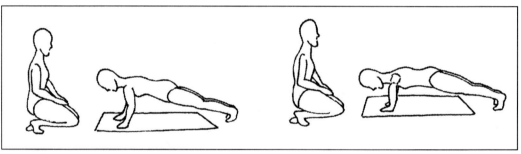

Figure A

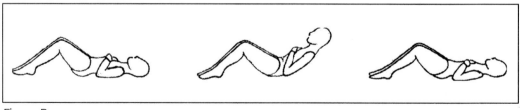

Figure B

*You or your coach/instructor may vary the evaluation standards to be more specific to your particular cheer needs.

#34: Graphing Your Cheer-Fitness Results— Your Cheer-Fitness Profile

Objective: To evaluate and graph all your cheer fitness test results from Tip #21 through Tip #33

Equipment Needed: A computer with graphics/spreadsheet package, or paper and a pen

Description: After you have evaluated your current cheer fitness abilities by completing Tip #21 through Tip #33, you should develop your cheer fitness profile by comparing how you performed on all the tests, and make a graph of your results. Use the space below to determine if you are physically ready to engage in cheer activities, and can perform them at acceptable levels that will help make your cheer experiences safer and more pleasant. Remember: learn to recognize your cheer-fitness strengths (and maintain them), while working to improve your weaknesses. At this point, rank how you performed on each test (#21 through #33) in categories like success (you achieved your goal), you came close to your goal (but need more work), or you failed to accomplish your goal (you need a lot more work).

Use the following abbreviations for each fitness test to help you graph your results in the allotted space.

- Agility (A)
- Balance (B)
- Coordination (C)
- Core stability (CS)

- Speed (S)
- Power (P)
- Reaction time (RT)
- Aerobic fitness (AF)

- Muscular strength (MS)
- Muscular endurance (ME)
- Flexibility (F)
- Body composition (BC)

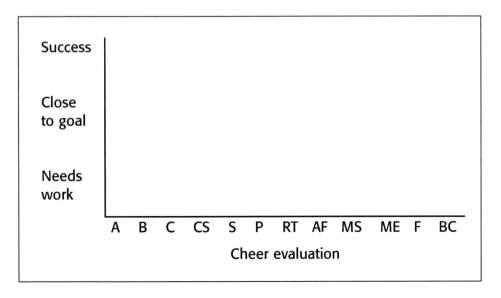

4

Training Smart: The Basics

Ronald Martinez/Getty Images

#35: Parts of a Sound Cheer-Training Program

Objective: To learn the basic ingredients of developing a sound cheer-training program for yourself and anyone else you might mentor

Equipment Needed: A pen and paper, a computer, and your cheer journal

Description: Developing a sound cheer-training program requires that you understand that you should employ exercise-science principles (the science of cheer training) as a foundation for your program, and that you learn how your body responds to the demands placed on it by your training (the art of cheer training). Successful cheerleading requires that you use both the science and art (application) of training. The following factors should be part of your individual and school/club cheer-training program, and will be covered individually in this chapter.

The Science of Cheer Training

- MVPA—moderate to vigorous physical activity
- Warm-up—activities that get you ready to cheer
- Cool-down—activities that help you recover from cheering
- FITT—the frequency, intensity, time, and type of cheer training you do
- Cheer effort rating scale—how hard or easy you think you are working
- Workout—the components of a quality cheer-training program, and how they should be organized to help you improve. Your workout should specifically focus on MVPA, cheer skills, resistance training (such as push-ups, pull-ups, weight training), and flexibility training.

The Art of Cheer Training

- Progression—how quickly do you change your FITT
- Trainability—how quickly can you improve with training and what is your potential to improve
- Overtraining—doing too much cheer training, such that it results in a negative effect on your cheerleading performance
- Detraining—loss of your cheer-fitness levels once you stop training
- Restoration—ways in which you can speed up your recovery from workout to workout
- Adherence—refers to your ability to stick with your cheer-training plan

Having learned about the basic ingredients of a sound cheer-training program, record your thoughts and develop a format to track your training efforts in your cheer journal.

#36: Cheering and MVPA

Objective: To learn what is meant by MVPA, and why you will need to participate regularly in MVPA to improve your cheer performance and maintain your good health

Equipment Needed: A pen and paper, a computer, and your cheer journal

Description: As you learned in Tip #5: What Talents and Skills Do You Need to Develop to Be Successful at Cheering?, MVPA stands for moderate-to-vigorous physical activity. Your cheer workouts will require large amounts of MVPA. But remember: you do not always have to work at your highest intensities to improve. Sometimes, participating in moderate activity is better than working "all out" to maintain your fitness levels. Following are examples of MVPA and how you can monitor your intensity levels.

Moderate Intensity Physical Activity or Exercise

- Examples of moderate activities and exercise include: walking briskly, cheer warm-ups, dancing, swimming, doing one or two sets of 10-to-12 repetitions of weight-training exercises with a relatively easy level of resistance for seven or eight major muscle groups, and cycling on level terrain.
- In these types activities you are starting to sweat, feel relatively warmer, and breathe harder, but you can still talk comfortably and are burning 3.5-to-7 calories per minute (for example, you burn one calorie per minute when you are sitting at rest).

Vigorous-Intensity Physical Activity or Exercise

- Examples of vigorous activities and exercise include: jogging, cheer-competition routines, high-impact aerobic dance, swimming continuous laps, performing three-to-five sets of 6-to-10 repetitions of strength-training exercise at a level of near muscular fatigue for 10-to-12 major muscle areas, and cycling uphill.
- At this level, you will be sweating and breathing hard, and you will be burning more than seven calories per minute (i.e., seven times your caloric burn rate when you are sitting at rest).

Recently, an expert panel of youth and adolescent exercise scientists recommended that school-aged youth should participate in 60 minutes of MVPA for good health that includes benefits for weight control, heart health, metabolic health, blood pressure health, mental health, self-esteem, academic performance, and bone health. Remember to get regular MVPA—even after your cheer days are over. Not only will it make you feel better, it will also make you look better. Drag along your family members regularly so they get their regular MVPA, too.

Having learned about the concept of MVPA, designate moderate or vigorous next to the activities you do in your cheer workouts in your cheer journal, and keep track of your MVPA minutes to see if you meet the goal of 60 minutes of MVPA per day.

#37: Your Cheer Warm-Up and Cool-Down

Objective: To learn the basic ingredients of an effective cheer warm-up and cool-down

Equipment Needed: A pen and paper, a computer, and your cheer journal

Description: Warm-up refers to activities that get you ready to cheer, and a cool-down refers to activities that help you recover from the demands you place on your body while cheering. Warming up before you cheer helps you increase your body temperature slightly and increase the level of blood flow to your working muscles (legs and arms). Cooling down after you do a cheer workout helps you recover gradually from exercising and helps prevent blood from pooling in your lower body (lower torso and legs), which can cause you to get dizzy and faint. You should adhere to the following warm-up and cool-down guidelines before and after (respectively) all cheer sessions.

Warm-Up

- Begin by doing some MVPA (brisk walking, slow jogging, stationary cycle, etc.) for about 5-to-10 minutes.
- Do seven or eight of the common cheer stretches and/or some calisthenics (as shown in Tip #38: Common Cheer Stretches) for approximately five minutes. If you have an injury, make sure you stretch and warm up the muscles around the affected area a little more than usual.
- Remember to warm up your upper and lower body, because you use all of your muscles when cheerleading.

Cool-Down

- Do some MVPA activities at a low-to-moderate level for five minutes at the end of a cheer workout until your heart rate drops below 100 bpm (beats per minute), or until you feel that your heart rate and breathing rate are almost back to their resting levels.
- When you feel that you are close to returning to your resting level of heart rate and breathing, do about 5-to-10 minutes of stretching to enhance your level of flexibility, and to minimize muscle stiffness.
- Remember to cool down after every cheer workout to optimize your cheer training.

Having learned about the basic ingredients of an effective cheer warm-up and cool-down, evaluate the warm-up and cool-down activities you have been doing in your cheer training. Record your thoughts in your cheer journal. Are your warm-up and cool-down activities effective, or do they need to be modified? If so, how should you modify them?

#38: Common Cheer Stretches

Objective: To learn about basic cheer stretches that you should include in your warm-up and cool-down cheer routines

Equipment Needed: A free, open space, preferably with a cheer mat

Description: This Tip requires you to perform the stretches provided by your cheer coach after a five-minute MVPA warm-up (see Tip #36: Cheering and MVPA). These stretches may include the following: side stretch, chest and arm stretch, trunk twist, reverse hurdle, shoulder shrug, side lunge, forward lunge, butterfly, and wall stretch. Practice each stretch very slowly at first. Then, once you feel comfortable doing each stretch, perform the stretch routine for 5-to-10 minutes, holding each stretch without bouncing.

Example of forward lunge stretch

Example of trunk-twist stretch

Example of side-stretch exercise

#39: Your Cheer FITT

Objective: To learn about the tools that will help you monitor your cheer FITT

Equipment Needed: A pen and paper, a computer, and your cheer journal

Description: As you learned in Tip #34: Graphing Your Cheer Fitness Results, FITT stands for frequency, intensity, time, and type. You should record your FITT score daily in your cheer journal so that you can follow your training progress and track how your body is responding to training (the art of cheer training). This step also enables you to evaluate how well you are adhering to sound exercise-science principles (the science of cheer training) as a foundation for your program. Use the following guidelines to enter your FITT score into your cheer journal for your daily MVPA (see Tip #35: Parts of a Sound Cheer Training Program) and cheer activities.

- **Frequency**—Try to get MVPA daily or on most days by either working out on your own or attending cheer workouts (or both). Be careful not to overtrain or do too much cheer-related activity, or you might see negative results.
- **Intensity**—Use your measured heart rate (HR) during your MVPA activities to determine your intensity of effort or utilize the following cheer-rating scale to rate your level of intensity. To determine your MVPA HR, you should use a commercial heart-rate monitor (i.e., a Polar™ monitor) or learn to take your pulse to estimate your MVPA HR. Most of your daily cheer workouts will require an intensity between 3 and 7, unless you are competing or working at a very high skill level. And remember: you do not (and *should not*) have to work at a high level of intensity every day to improve.

Cheer Effort Rating Scale
(Rate your daily workout on a scale from 0-to-10)
0—no MVPA, rest
1—slow walking, cheer stretching activities
2—between 1 and 3
3—activity like brisk walking, cheer MVPA warm-up drills, HR < 130 beats/minute
4—between 3 and 5
5—cheer workout with MVPA for 30 minutes, HR ~ 130-to-140 beats/minute
6—between 5 and 7
7—cheer workout with MVPA for 60 minutes, HR > 160 beats/minute
8—between 7 and 9
9—cheer workout with MVPA for > 90 minutes or cheer competition with more than one performance per day, HR > 180 beats/minute
10—one of the hardest cheer workouts you've ever had

- **Time**—Try to get a minimum of 225 minutes of cheer MVPA per week unless you are ill, injured, or have another health-related reason to limit your MVPA.
- **Type**—Try to get a variety of MVPA daily. Include regular stretching for maintaining and/or increasing your flexibility, and resistance work (such as push-ups, curl-ups, or weightlifting activities) to maintain and/or improve your strength, muscular endurance, and explosive power to your MVPA efforts.

Having learned how to record your FITT effectively, begin documenting this information in your cheer journal.

#40: Your Cheer Workout

Objective: To learn about the basic components of a quality cheer workout

Equipment Needed: A pen and paper, a computer, and your cheer journal

Description: A quality cheer workout includes several components. As such, you should design your personal workouts using the guidelines noted below. You should also encourage your fellow cheerleaders to include all of the listed components in their workouts to optimize their training as well.

The Components of a Cheer Workout		
Component	Type of Activities	Time and Frequency per Week
Warm-up	MVPA (see #37), cheer stretches, and calisthenics	10–15 minutes, preferably daily
Specific cheer	MVPA conditioning,	20–90 minutes total, preferably daily
Focus activities	Resistance conditioning, flexibility, cheer-specific drills (like tumbling, jumps, motions, etc.)	(4–8 exercises, 2–3 times per week 7–8 stretches, preferably daily)
Cool-down	MVPA (see #37), cheer stretches, and calisthenics	10–15 minutes, preferably daily

Having learned about the components of a quality cheer workout, design or evaluate a sample workout you want to do (or have already done) in your cheer journal.

#41: Your Cheer Resistance Training

Objective: To learn about what your resistance-training workouts should consist of, and how your cheer abilities will be improved by performing resistance training

Equipment Needed: A pen and paper, a computer, your cheer journal, and access to resistance equipment that is appropriate to your needs

Description: Your cheer resistance-training program should be focused on developing muscular strength, muscular endurance, and explosive power. Specifically, you need to be strong and agile for your own body weight and performance level (base versus flyer, etc.). Resistance training for cheerleading includes weightlifting, body resistance, plyometrics (or bounding, jump drills), and alternative options, like resistance-band training. Your cheer resistance-training program should be designed with the concept of FITT in mind. For example, you should engage in resistance training two-to-three times per week. Your intensity level should usually be 50-to-80 percent of your maximum lifting ability, which can be determined by your cheer coach. The time (duration) you exercise will be based upon on how many repetitions of a movement you do and the amount of rest you take between exercises or sets of repetitions (usually 30 seconds to one minute). The type of exercise will be based on which resistance exercise you are doing.

Four of the more common methods of resistance training are weightlifting, body-resistance training, plyometric training, and resistance-band training. Each approach has its own advantages and limitations.

- **Weightlifting**—To engage in this type of program, you need access to free weights (weight bars and weight plates) or strength-training machines. Many cheerleaders (especially bases) engage in weightlifting to increase their levels of strength, core stability, muscular endurance, and explosiveness. You should have your cheer coach or a school coach with weightlifting experience help you learn to lift weights safely and effectively. Beginning weightlifting programs (typically designed for individuals ages 12-to-14 years) should focus more on lighter weights and more repetitions, while advanced programs (normally for those who are over 14 years of age) may involve using heavier weights and performing fewer repetitions.

- **Body-resistance training**—If you do not have access to weight equipment, you can perform exercises like push-ups, pull-ups, sit-ups, and tumbling drills that force you to move your own body weight through a particular range of motion. Such exercises can be performed in the traditional way (lowering and raising your body through the desired range of motion or in negative-only fashion (lowering your body only) if you can't raise your body to the "up position" during the exercise.

- **Plyometrics**—These activities are designed to stretch and contract your muscles very rapidly to increase your level of cheer explosiveness. Plyometrics can take many forms, but usually involve in-place jumping, lunges, hops and bounds, skipping, and box jumps. Properly done, plyometric exercises are appropriate for individuals of all ages and fitness levels. Have your cheer coach or a school coach help you develop a safe and effective plyometric program.

- **Resistance-band training**—You can use elastic bands or latex tubing to help you develop your levels of cheer strength, core stability, muscular endurance, and explosiveness. Usually color-coded for intensity (or resistance level), resistance bands are available at most sporting goods stores.

Having learned about resistance training for cheer, design a basic cheer resistance-training program for yourself, and record it in your cheer journal.

#42: Your Cheer Flexibility Training

Objective: To learn about what your flexibility-training workouts should consist of, and how your cheer abilities will be improved by performing regular flexibility training

Equipment Needed: A pen and paper, a computer, and your cheer journal (access to a cheer mat is also recommended)

Description: Your flexibility-training program should be focused on optimizing your level of total body flexibility. Specifically, you need to be flexible in order to move your entire body weight through whatever range of motion your cheer activities involve. Flexibility training for cheerleading includes static stretches, ballistic or plyometric stretches, and partner-assisted stretches. Your cheer flexibility-training program should be designed with the concept of FITT in mind. For example, the frequency of your workouts should be five times per week minimum. The intensity level of your regimen should be to the point of slight stretch discomfort (but not painful). The time (duration) of your flexibility-training session will be based upon on the type of stretch and your experience. As a rule, all stretches should be held for 30-to-60 seconds to increase your range of motion. The type of training will be based on which flexibility exercise you are doing. Once you have read the following definitions, design a basic cheer flexibility-training program for yourself, and record it in your cheer journal.

- **Static stretches**—These stretches are slow, smooth, and in a prolonged manner. A static stretch would be like reaching down while standing and touching your toes without bouncing.

- **Ballistic (or plyometric) stretches**—These stretches involve quick up-and-down or side-to-side bobbing movements that are held only briefly. Ballistic stretches are important to include in your regular cheer training, but should only be done after a good warm-up and some static stretching of all of your body parts that you will utilize in your cheer activities.

- **Partner-assisted stretching**—This type of exercise involves stretching against a counterforce like a partner, a chair, or a towel. In this type of stretch, you would move in a range of motion, while your partner (or the chair or towel) provides resistance. An example of this type of stretch would be your partner pushing on the bottom of your feet towards you as you sit on the floor and lean forward to touch your toes, while keeping your legs straight.

Example of a static stretch

#43: Your Cheer Progression and Training

Objective: To learn about factors that can influence your cheer-training progression and development

Equipment Needed: A pen and paper, a computer, and your cheer journal

Description: The progression of your cheer-training program refers to how often you should change your FITT. Usually, you should change your FITT gradually as you get in better shape. You should listen to your body and not increase your FITT if you are always tired and sore from your current cheer FITT level. You should never increase all the FITT factors or any one of them too fast or too soon, since doing so can increase your risks for an overuse injury (see Tip #12: Common Cheer Injuries and Risks). You should adhere to the following stages and factors of cheer progression and training to help you with developing the art of adjusting your FITT. After you have read the information, record your cheer progression in your cheer journal.

Stages of Cheer Progression and Training

Initial stage (Weeks 0-8)—Quick improvements in fitness and skills often occur

Improvement stage (Weeks 9-24)—Improvements are continuing, but occur more gradually

Maintenance stage (Weeks 24+)—Your FITT is held constant

Relapse stage—You stop training, which could be a normal event due to illness, injury, or boredom. Hopefully, however, you recover relatively quickly from whatever factor(s) caused you to relapse and begin participating in regular MVPA again, for your good health, if nothing else.

Factors Influencing Your Cheer Progression and Training

Your initial fitness level—Usually, the less fit you are to start, the greater and faster the gains you will experience with training.

Your heredity—Pick your parents well, because it always helps to have talent.

The rate at which you change your FITT—Remember that determining the appropriate FITT is an art to training, and you will have to learn how to change your FITT according to how quickly your body can adapt to cheer training.

Your specific goals—You should focus on improving your cheer skills, while maintaining your good health.

#44: Your Cheer Trainability

Objective: To learn about factors that can influence your cheer trainability

Equipment Needed: A pen and paper, a computer, and your cheer journal

Description: As was noted previously, your trainability is how quickly you can improve with your cheer training and your potential for improvement. Your trainability is generally based on your heredity (anywhere from 30-to-50 percent for most cheer skills), but participation in a sound, scientific-based cheer-training program can help you improve your cheer abilities—even if you have less initial skill than someone else. As you learned in Tip #43: Your Cheer Progression and Training, you will go through stages of improvement with your cheer training. Each person on your cheer team will change or adapt to training differently during your training season. Some teammates will improve very rapidly, while others may struggle. Eventually, everyone will most likely experience a leveling off in their performance or fitness levels. This leveling off of performance or fitness is called a plateau, and it is a natural part of training. The plateau effect indicates that you may need to increase or decrease your FITT to see future improvements. It may also mean that you are reaching your peak ability for one specific cheer skill or type of cheer fitness.

Having learned about the cheer-trainability principle, graph your cheer-training progress and determine if you have hit any training plateaus. Remember, if you have hit a plateau, it is normal, and you probably need to adjust your FITT to see future improvement.

#45: Cheer Overtraining

Objective: To learn about factors that can influence cheer overtraining

Equipment Needed: A pen and paper, a computer, and your cheer journal

Description: As was noted previously, overtraining is doing too much training such that your cheerleading performance is negatively affected. Overtraining also can result if you do not get enough rest (or restoration) following training. On occasion, it can lead to abnormal levels of physical and mental stress or burnout. The following symptoms or conditions are associated with overtraining, and you should become familiar with them:

Symptoms or Conditions Associated With Cheer Overtraining

- Constant fatigue that lasts for several days to weeks
- Insomnia, or trouble sleeping, especially when you are tired
- Constant muscle soreness—you ache all the time
- Rapid weight loss—more than five pounds in a week
- Loss of appetite—too tired to eat
- Elevated resting heart rate (around 10 beats above your normal resting levels when you first awake)
- Sick constantly, especially with upper-respiratory (lung) infections
- Exercise addiction—cheer exercise and/or practice becomes more important than family, friends, work, or other important aspects of life
- Eating disorders—not eating enough calories to meet your daily needs, or eating and purging, which reduces the number of calories absorbed by the body

Preventing Cheer Overtraining

- Recognize the signs of overtraining *early*, and share your feelings with your cheer coach and family.
- Optimize your recovery (or restoration) from cheer exercise (see Tip #47: Your Cheer Restoration).
- Take regular breaks from cheer training whenever possible (for a week or more). During breaks, practice good eating and MVPA habits, but relax from the stresses of competition.
- Get professional counseling if you are suffering from a eating disorder, or if you are addicted to cheer exercise and/or practice.

Having learned about the cheer overtraining principle, review your cheer journal to determine if you have ever suffered the signs of overtraining. Record how you can prevent cheer overtraining in the future.

#46: Your Cheer Detraining

Objective: To learn about factors that can influence your cheer detraining

Equipment Needed: A pen and paper, a computer, and your cheer journal

Description: As was previously noted, detraining is the loss of your cheer-fitness levels once you stop training. Detraining does not occur in a day, two days, or even three. In fact, it is specific to each of your cheer-fitness abilities. Skipping a day or two of cheer training is even wise when you are unusually tired, sick, or injured. The following facts and recommendations about detraining will help you better understand how to cope with detraining, and minimize the potential negative effects it may have on your cheering:

Facts and Recommendations About Cheer Detraining

- It takes about 10 days of complete detraining (no MVPA) to lose half of what you have you gained in training involving your aerobic fitness level (or cardiovascular fitness).
- It takes about 20 days or more of complete detraining (no MVPA and no resistance training) to lose half of what you gained in training involving your muscular endurance levels.
- It takes about 30 days or more of complete detraining (no MVPA and no resistance training) to lose half of what you gained in training involving your muscular strength levels.
- Even if you have to detrain due to overtraining, sickness, or injury, you can maintain minimal levels of cheer fitness by cross-training, performing MVPA at low levels, or by following a sound rehabilitation program provided by your coach, athletic trainer, or physician.

   Having learned about the cheer detraining principle, review your cheer journal to recall any periods of detraining you may have experienced. Record how you can cope with cheer detraining in the future.

#47: Your Cheer Restoration

Objective: To learn about factors that can influence your cheer restoration

Equipment Needed: A pen and paper, a computer, and your cheer journal

Description: As was noted previously, restoration refers to the ways in which you can speed up your recovery from workout to workout. Your ability to recover quickly from your cheer workouts depends on your FITT. If you are working at high levels of intensity, frequency, or have short time periods to recover from MVPA, you will need to adjust your restoration time or increase your risks for overtraining, sickness, and injury. The following factors are related to optimizing your cheer restoration:

Factors That Influence Your Cheer Restoration

- *Fitness level*—The less fit you are, usually the longer it takes to recover.
- *Experience*—Usually, the more experienced you are, the faster you can recover.
- *Environment*—The more extreme the environmental conditions (especially high heat and humidity), the longer it takes to recover.
- *Amount of rest*—A cheerleader-in-training needs to get 8-to-10 hours of sleep, on average, to improve her restoration. Less sleep results in less recovery.
- *Nutrition (including fluids)*—What you eat and drink and before, during, and after cheer MVPA can influence your restoration (see Chapter 5 for more information on restoration).

Having learned about the cheer-restoration principle, review your cheer journal to determine if you are optimizing your cheer restoration. Record how you can improve your cheer restoration in the future.

#48: Your Cheer Training Adherence

Objective: To learn about factors that can influence your cheer adherence

Equipment Needed: A pen and paper, a computer, and your cheer journal

Description: As was noted previously, adherence refers to your ability to stick with your cheer-training plan. As you can imagine, several factors might have positive or negative effects on your cheer adherence. The following factors can affect your level of cheer adherence:

Factors That Influence Your Cheer Adherence

- *Lack of time*—Investigate how to use time-management skills to optimize your daily school, social, family, and cheer time.
- *Poor cheer fitness levels*—Remember: always do enough MVPA to at least maintain your cheer-fitness levels.
- *Unrealistic goals or expectations*—Review your goals regularly with your coach, and adjust them as necessary, based upon your progress.
- *Illness or injury*—Optimize your restoration strategies for recovering from illness (follow your physician's advice, and take all medications as specified), and obtain and follow a rehabilitation plan from your coach, athletic trainer, or physician to help you recover from your injury.
- *Competitive stress*—Remember that cheer training and competition normally cause stress, which can come from within yourself or from teammates, coaches, parents, etc. Learn to cope with competitive stress by being positive, staying on task, being humble, and enjoying each day you get to cheer.

Having learned about the cheer-adherence principle, review your cheer journal to determine if you are optimizing your level of cheer adherence. Record how you can improve your cheer adherence in the future.

5

Nutrition, Eating, and Controlling Your Body Weight to Compete

#49: Factors That Influence Your Cheer Diet

Objective: To learn about various influences on your cheer food choices

Equipment Needed: A pen and paper, a computer, and your cheer journal

Description: Have you thought about how your cheer diet might help or hurt your cheerleading performances? This chapter reviews a number of important facts and tips to optimize your cheer diet to improve your cheer experiences.

Why do you eat the way you do? What factors cause you to make good or poor dietary decisions? Make a list of the following factors that you think influence how you eat and how you might change your cheer eating behavior for the better. Enter your results in your cheer journal.

- *Your nutrition knowledge*—How much do you now about proper cheer nutrition? You can positively influence your cheer nutrition (and performances) by learning how to eat better by choosing and eating healthy.
- *Culture*—Your family's customs, traditions, and beliefs may influence your eating behaviors in small or large ways.
- *Friends*—Your friends may be the most important influence on your current dietary practices, which may be good or may require adjusting if they influence you to eat poorly.
- *Hunger and appetite*—Your need to eat foods for energy (hunger) and your desire to eat (appetite), which is more psychological, are strong influences on your eating habits.
- *Emotions*—Your feelings can cause to you to overeat or eat too little.
- *Advertising*—You are exposed to numerous ads that tell what, when, and where to eat. Remember: advertising can either be good or bad as far as influencing your cheer nutrition.
- *Time and convenience*—You may be pressed for time because of a busy lifestyle, causing you to depend on trying to eat quickly and cheaply, which is easy to do with all the fast food choices in our society. However, if you do not make good food choices, you undoubtedly are not optimizing your cheer diet.

#50: Your Cheer Food Guide Pyramid

Objective: To learn about the recommended dietary guidelines for Americans and "my pyramid," and to learn how to read food labels

Equipment Needed: A pen and paper, a computer with an Internet connection, and your cheer journal

Description: It is absolutely critical that you learn about eating healthy to help improve your cheerleading success. In order to get started, you need to go online and check out two websites that you should bookmark for future reference for doing all you can do to "eat to compete." The first site is www.mypyramid.gov, and the second is www.nutrition.gov. Both sites can help you understand the latest dietary guidelines for Americans and how you can design a sound nutritional program that is appropriate for your needs and interests.

Tips for Navigating www.mypyramid.gov

- On the home page, enter your individual data for your age, gender, and the amount of daily MVPA you are currently getting. Hit "*submit*," and you'll see a personal eating plan developed for you.
- The plan you receive will highlight the number of calories that you need from foods and liquids each day (for example, you need a minimum of 1440 calories per day if you do no MVPA).
- Your dietary plan will also highlight how many ounces of grains, vegetables, fruits, milk, and meat and beans you should consume each day.
- Your dietary plan will also provide you with some extra daily tips about eating a variety of veggies, fats, and sugars.
- The site will provide you with several options to view, print, and learn more about nutrition.
- Finally, you can click on the "*subjects*" icon to get detailed information about your pyramid and how the guidelines have been developed.

Tips for Navigating www.nutrition.gov

- On the home page, browse for information by audience and select "*teens*." You will get information about several nutritional topics, including "Smart Nutrition 101."
- Click on the icons of interest to you, and if you have a printer, you may want to download the information for future reference.
- You can also search topics that are in the news from the home page.
- Finally, you can cross-reference back to "*my pyramid*" food information.

Having learned about the cheer food-guide pyramid, start keeping a log of your dietary habits in your cheer journal, and review it regularly to help maintain your weight in a healthy range.

GRAINS	VEGETABLES	FRUITS	MILK	MEAT & BEANS
Make half your grains whole	Vary your veggies	Focus on fruits	Get your calcium-rich foods	Go lean with protein
Eat at least 3 oz. of whole-grain cereals, breads, crackers, rice, or pasta every day 1 oz. is about 1 slice of bread, about 1 cup of breakfast cereal, or ½ cup of cooked rice, cereal, or pasta	Eat more dark-green veggies like broccoli, spinach, and other dark leafy greens Eat more orange vegetables like carrots and sweetpotatoes Eat more dry beans and peas like pinto beans, kidney beans, and lentils	Eat a variety of fruit Choose fresh, frozen, canned, or dried fruit Go easy on fruit juices	Go low-fat or fat-free when you choose milk, yogurt, and other milk products If you don't or can't consume milk, choose lactose-free products or other calcium sources such as fortified foods and beverages	Choose low-fat or lean meats and poultry Bake it, broil it, or grill it Vary your protein routine — choose more fish, beans, peas, nuts, and seeds

For a 2,000-calorie diet, you need the amounts below from each food group. To find the amounts that are right for you, go to MyPyramid.gov.

Eat 6 oz. every day	Eat 2½ cups every day	Eat 2 cups every day	Get 3 cups every day; for kids aged 2 to 8, it's 2	Eat 5½ oz. every day

Find your balance between food and physical activity
- Be sure to stay within your daily calorie needs.
- Be physically active for at least 30 minutes most days of the week.
- About 60 minutes a day of physical activity may be needed to prevent weight gain.
- For sustaining weight loss, at least 60 to 90 minutes a day of physical activity may be required.
- Children and teenagers should be physically active for 60 minutes every day, or most days.

Know the limits on fats, sugars, and salt (sodium)
- Make most of your fat sources from fish, nuts, and vegetable oils.
- Limit solid fats like butter, stick margarine, shortening, and lard, as well as foods that contain these.
- Check the Nutrition Facts label to keep saturated fats, trans fats, and sodium low.
- Choose food and beverages low in added sugars. Added sugars contribute calories with few, if any, nutrients.

MyPyramid.gov
STEPS TO A HEALTHIER YOU

USDA

U.S. Department of Agriculture
Center for Nutrition Policy and Promotion
April 2005
CNPP-15

#51: Your Cheer Energy Needs

Objective: To learn about balancing the amounts of calories you need to eat with the calories you liberate (or burn) by engaging in MVPA

Equipment Needed: A computer with an Internet connection and your cheer journal

Description: According to Leslie Bonci, MPH, RD, the director of sports medicine at the University of Pittsburgh Medical Center, you can optimize cheer safety and performance in several ways by eating smart. In fact, your diet can affect all of the following:

- Your strength
- Your speed
- Your stamina
- Your mental concentration
- Your mood
- Your recovery

Bonci also noted that busy lifestyles often lead to poor eating practices, and that cheerleaders often do not know what to eat, when to eat, how much to eat, how to prepare foods, what to choose when eating out, and what are the legitimate benefits and limitations of food supplements. Do you? The next several Tips in this chapter will explore the dietary concerns raised by Bonci.

One of the most important parts of your cheer diet should be balancing the amounts of calories you need to eat with the calories you liberate (or burn) by engaging in MVPA. On average, physically active teen males need 20-to-25 calories per pound of body weight daily, while teen females need 15-to-20 calories per pound of body weight daily. For example, a teen female who weighs 100 pounds requires 1500-to-2000 calories per day. Your calorie intake should increase during intense cheer training and in the early stages of training to meet your additional energy needs. In order to get all the calories you need daily, you probably should eat more than three meals a day. In fact, Bonci recommends that teens eat smaller, more frequent meals (e.g., consume a meal within one hour after waking and then an additional meal every three-to-four hours). Learning how to match the number of calories you consume with the number you liberate can help you prevent you from feeling fatigued and potentially overtraining.

At www.mypyramid.gov, use the my pyramid "tracker" function to de-termine how many calories you should be consuming, and track your caloric intake and expenditure for three days or more to see if you are meeting your daily needs. Record your results in your cheer journal.

#52: Your Cheer Carbohydrate Dietary Needs

Objective: To learn about the importance of consuming the proper amount of carbohydrates in your daily diet to enhance your cheer performance

Equipment Needed: A computer with an Internet connection and your cheer journal

Description: Carbohydrates are starches and sugars that exist in food. Simple carbohydrates are found in fruits, candy, cookies, and sodas. Complex carbohydrates are found in foods like vegetables, breads, cereals, pasta, rice, and beans. It is best to consume more complex carbs than simple ones, because they are absorbed more slowly by your body and contain more vitamins. Dietary fiber (like grains, stems, roots, nuts, seeds, and fruit coverings) is found in complex carbohydrates. All factors considered, foodstuffs that contain dietary fiber are healthy for you to consume for good digestive health.

Carbs are your body's main source of fuel for day-to-day living and cheering, providing you with four calories of energy per gram. They should make up about 50-to-60 percent of your daily calories. For example, a teen female who weighs 100 pounds and who needs 1500-to-2000 total calories per day would need 750-to-1000 calories of carbohydrates in her daily nutrition plan. Remember: if you do not eat enough carbohydrates, you will most likely compromise your cheer performance. The following table contains foods high in carbohydrates from a variety of sources:

Grains	Fruits	Vegetables	Milk Sources
Bagels	Apples	Carrots	Yogurt
Bread	Bananas	Corn	Milk (2% or less)
Cereals	Fruit juices	Green beans	Cheese
Pasta noodles	Oranges	Potatoes	Pudding
Popcorn	Pears	Broccoli	

Use the my pyramid "tracker" function at www.mypyramid.gov to determine how many calories from carbohydrates you are consuming daily. Record your results in your cheer journal.

#53: Your Cheer Protein and Fat Dietary Needs

Objective: To learn about the importance of consuming the appropriate amount of protein and fats in your daily diet to enhance your cheer performance

Equipment Needed: A computer with an Internet connection and your cheer journal

Description: Proteins are nutrients that are important for your body's growth and repair. Similar to carbohydrates, they also provide you with four calories of energy per gram. Although proteins can provide you with some fuel for your energy needs, they are not used nearly as much for energy by your body as carbohydrates and fats. Proteins should make up 10-to-15 percent of your daily dietary needs. For example, a teen female who weighs 100 pounds and who needs 1500-to-2000 total calories per day would need about 150-to-200 calories of proteins in her daily nutrition plan. Remember: if you do not eat enough or too much protein in your daily diet, you most likely will compromise your cheer performance.

Fats are nutrients that are high in energy, help you absorb vitamins like A, D, E, and K, and help make you feel satisfied because they take longer to digest than either carbs or proteins. Fats are important to consume in your cheer diet because they also help control a hormone in your body called testosterone, which is used to build body tissues. Fats provide you with nine calories of energy per gram, but are harder to break down at higher MVPA intensities than carbs. Fats should make up about 30 percent of your daily dietary needs (but no less than 20 percent, because you will lower your testosterone levels). For example, a teen female who weighs 100 pounds and who needs 1500-to-2000 total calories per day would need about 450-to-600 calories of fats in her daily nutrition plan. Remember: if you do not eat enough or too much fat in your daily diet, you most likely will compromise your cheer performance.

Use the following dietary tips as a guide to consuming proteins and fats in your daily cheer diet:
- Foods high in protein include meats, fish, chicken, eggs, cheese, and milk.
- Protein from meat sources is better than from plant sources because it contains ample amounts of all essential amino acids, while vegetable proteins do not.
- If you are a vegetarian who avoids meat, eggs, and milk products, you need to eat a wide variety of plant foods to meet your protein needs and should consider getting guidance from a trained professional to help ensure that you consume a balanced diet.

- Eating too many fats in your diet can cause weight gain that may be unhealthful and increase your risk for health problems such as type II diabetes (a high blood-sugar problem).
- Eat only about 10 percent of your daily fat calories from animal fats, including butter and lard.
- Choose foods that are lower in fat, like cooked dry beans, peas, fish, leaner meats, and chicken.

Use the my pyramid "tracker" function at www.mypyramid.gov to determine how many calories from proteins and fats you should are consuming daily. Record your results in your cheer journal.

#54: Your Cheer Calcium, Iron, and Salt Dietary Needs

Objective: To learn about the importance of consuming the recommended amount of calcium, iron, and salt (sodium) in your daily diet to enhance your cheer performance

Equipment Needed: A computer with an Internet connection and your cheer journal

Description: Calcium, iron, and sodium are important minerals that you need to include in your daily diet to enhance your cheerleading performance and to help maintain your good health. You need numerous other minerals in your diet, but this Tip focuses on these three, and how you can avoid common cheer health problems related to diet deficient in calcium, iron, and sodium.

Calcium

Calcium is an essential factor in building and maintaining strong bones for cheering, and for your future health. In your teen years, because your bones are growing, you should make sure you get plenty of calcium in your diet by consuming dairy products (milk, cheese, and yogurt), and dark green, leafy vegetables. If you do not eat a diet rich in calcium, you may need to take calcium supplements if recommended by your doctor to meet your dietary needs. Your cheer training, which includes jumping and bounding, will also help make your bones strong if you get the calcium you need in your diet. The combination of good calcium intake and your cheer MVPA may help you prevent or delay the problems that can occur later in life with osteoporosis (brittle, weak bones).

Iron

Iron is important for your body to maintain the right amount of hemoglobin (the substance in your red blood cells that carries oxygen to your muscles) for cheering, and to help you avoid iron-deficiency anemia (i.e., low red blood cells and hemoglobin). Foods that are rich in iron include red meats, shellfish, poultry, eggs, beans, peanuts, and dried fruits. If you do not eat red meat and are a vegetarian, you may become deficient in iron, because animal sources of iron are more efficient sources for absorption by your body than plant sources. However, vegetarians can still get all the iron they need, if they eat a variety of iron-rich plant foods, like beans, peanuts, and dried fruits.

Sodium

Sodium (or salt) is a key factor in maintaining your body's fluid balance and for effective nerve stimulation of your muscles. You probably get all the sodium you need in your diet because many foods (especially fast foods) you may eat have high levels of sodium. However, if you happen to be a heavy sweater and lose a lot of salt (you can tell if you are because you will see lots of salt stains on your shirt), you may need to get more salt in your diet, which can help prevent cramping (see Tip #16: Preventing Heat Injuries). Remember to drink plenty of fluids, particularly when you consume foods that are higher in sodium content (read your food labels for sodium content). If your family avoids consuming sodium (no saltshakers on the table for those family members that might have high-blood pressure, for example), and you are a heavy sweater who needs more sodium to prevent muscle cramping, talk to your coach and physician to get professional advice about what you should do concerning your sodium and water intake.

Use the my pyramid "tracker" function at www.mypyramid.gov to determine if you are meeting your daily calcium, iron, and sodium needs. Record your results in your cheer journal.

#55: Your Cheer Fluid Dietary Needs

Objective: To learn about the importance of consuming the proper amount and types of fluids in your daily diet to enhance your cheer performance

Equipment Needed: A computer with an Internet connection and your cheer journal

Description: Having learned about taking in fluids in Tip #16: Preventing Heat Injuries, you may experience the following negative cheer-performance results, if you are not taking the right amount and right type of fluids:

- Decreased performance (strength, speed, endurance)
- Decreased mental ability to focus and willpower
- Decreased restoration (recovery time)
- Increased cheer effort rating (your involvement feels harder than it really is or should be)
- Increased body temperature, placing you at a higher risk for a heat injury
- Increased risk of injury

Use the following guidelines to optimize your daily fluid intake and cheer performance:

- Drink fluids like water and sports drinks more than sodas, energy drinks (those with caffeine or herbs), or milk during cheer training and competitions.
- Remember that sports drinks provide fuel, salt, and other minerals that water does not, but are probably unnecessary unless you are engaging in MVPA for longer than 30 minutes a time.
- Keep in mind that sports drinks are easy to digest, are flavored, which may cause you to drink more, and can help you recover faster from cheer MVPA.
- Weigh yourself before and after practice, and make sure you are close to your pre-practice weight (within one or two pounds) before you practice again.
- Observe the color of your urine. It should be clear or light yellow if you are properly hydrated (or are in fluid balance). If it is dark yellow, you are probably dehydrated and at a higher risk for a heat injury.
- Drink at least 9-to-10 glasses of water (sports drinks mixed in) per day, along with other servings of fluids.

Keep track of the amount and types of fluids that you consume daily for three days. Determine if you are meeting the general guidelines for fluid intake, and record your results in your cheer journal.

#56: Eating for Cheer Competitions

Objective: To learn about how you can eat to compete more successfully

Equipment Needed: A pen and paper, a computer with an Internet connection, and your cheer journal

Description: Have you thought about what you should eat and when you should eat before a cheer competition? If you have not, you should, because your pre-competition eating can have positive or negative influences on your individual and team cheer performances. Adhere to the following nutrition tips to improve your cheer pre-competition eating. Once you review the tips, evaluate how you might need to change your cheer pre-competition eating in the future, and record your results in your cheer journal.

- *Determine the kind of competition*—Some competitions are all-day events, while others may only include a 30-minute warm-up and a two-and-a-half-to-three-minute competition routine. You need to eat and consume fluids more wisely for longer competitions because you can run low on energy or get dehydrated if you do not. One or both situations can negatively influence your individual and team performance.
- *Focus on carbohydrates*—You should avoid foods high in fat or protein before competitions, because they will not supply you with as much energy as carbohydrates. Try to eat pasta, whole-grain breads, and rice prior to competition if you have time to digest them.
- *Think about timing*—It is best to allow three hours of digestion time after eating and prior to cheer competitions. However, if you only have an hour or two to eat before competing, you will want to eat something lighter, like fresh fruits, fruit juices, a sports drink or shake, or a muffin so that you have time to digest the foods and not feel full prior to competing—a situation that typically will compromise your level of performance.
- *Think about portion size*—You should avoid overeating during the pre-competition meal. Eat normal portions (like one helping).
- *Think digestion*—Only you will know the foods that you digest the best before competitions. Pay attention to what foods agree with you and which ones may not. Avoid foods that upset your stomach prior to cheer competitions.
- *Think about fluids*—You should drink fluids before, during, and after the competition to stay hydrated. Water is probably fine for short competitions, but for longer all-day events, you may want to use sport drinks to stay hydrated.
- *Think recovery*—Tip #57: Eating for Optimal Restoration for Cheering will provide you with more specifics about how to eat and drink to best recover from competition, but it is especially important to think about your cheer recovery strategies if you have to compete more than once in a day at a competition.
- *Search for more advice*—You can find more about eating to compete by searching for tips at www.mypyramid.gov and www.nutrition.gov.

#57: Eating for Optimal Restoration for Cheering

Objective: To learn about how you can eat to optimize your cheer restoration

Equipment Needed: A pen and paper, a computer with an Internet connection, and your cheer journal

Description: As was previously stated in Chapter 4, restoration refers to the ways in which you can speed up your recovery from workout to workout. One way to speed up your cheer restoration after a hard workout or competition so that you can train or compete again at your best is to pay attention to how you eat and drink immediately after your cheer efforts. Dr. John Ivy, an expert exercise physiologist at the University of Texas and co-author of *Nutrient Timing*, has studied ways to optimize athletic restoration. Use the following dietary tips from Dr. Ivy to improve your cheer restoration for training and/or multiple performances on competition days. Once you have reviewed the tips, evaluate how you might need to change your cheer restoration eating and drinking habits in the future, and record your results in your cheer journal.

Cheer Restoration Goals

- Replenish any fluids you may have lost, especially in a warm, outside environment (if possible), within 15-to-30 minutes after your cheer efforts. Water is good, but a sport drink may be better if you have worked hard for an hour or so or if you have to compete again during the same day.

- Re-supply your body's stock of carbohydrates and proteins with low-fat foods. Eat a small snack (if possible, within 30 minutes after your workout) that includes items like bagels, fruit yogurt, fruit juice, or pretzels.

- Avoid the snack bar or concession stands until after you have finished with your workout or competitions for the day. Always keep in mind that a valid reason exists concerning why junk foods are commonly referred to as "empty calories."

#58: Dietary Supplements and Cheering

Objective: To help you learn about national recommendations regarding the use of dietary supplements for MVPA activities like cheering

Equipment Needed: A pen and paper, a computer with an Internet connection, and your cheer journal

Description: It is estimated by experts that over one million teens use or have tried various dietary supplements to enhance their sports or MVPA performance. Dietary supplements include numerous substances, but this Tip focuses on caffeine, creatine, amino acids, herbal supplements, vitamins, and minerals. Among the primary reasons given for trying dietary supplements by teens are to meet extra demands of the activity, to respond to peer pressure, to obtain a cheerleader's "edge," and to make up for a sub-par dietary plan or dietary habits. Typically, it is not recommended that adolescents use dietary supplements unless they're recommended by a physician, because no studies have been conducted about their effects on performance in teens and because most research on their use has failed to document (confirm) their purported benefits. In fact, as a search on "dietary supplements" at www.nutrition.gov shows, dietary supplement use tends to have more questionable benefits versus any documented positive effects. Use the following information on dietary supplements to guide you in your cheer nutritional choices. Once you have reviewed the information, evaluate how you might need to change your current and future cheer eating habits, and record your results in your cheer journal.

Dietary Supplement

- *Caffeine*—stimulates the central nervous system, but can make you hyper, have headaches, get nervous, and become dehydrated. One or two caffeine drinks a day are probably okay, but more than that can negatively affect your cheer performance.
- *Creatine*—increases energy recovery in short-burst exercise. In reality, if you eat meat, you probably get all you need. Furthermore, its effects on growth and development in teens are unknown.
- *Amino acids*—are the building blocks of protein in your diet, but have not been shown to improve performance in adults. In addition, they are expensive and can cause your stomach to become upset.
- *Herbal supplements, vitamins, and minerals*—are shown to have limited benefits even when those taking them follow the recommendations listed on www.mypyamid.gov. Furthermore, most of these types of supplements are not regulated very rigorously by the governmental agencies—avoid complicating any decision concerning their possible use.

#59: Your Cheer Body Image and Weight Control

Objective: To help you learn about how your body image can influence your thoughts and methods of weight control

Equipment Needed: A pen and paper, a computer with an Internet connection, and your cheer journal

Description: The way you view or see your body is called your body image. Since cheerleading is an activity like gymnastics, figure skating, dance, and cross-country running, too much body weight can negatively influence your performance. However, you should also understand that being too lean might make you unhealthy and also have a negative impact on your cheer performance. The key issue is what can you do to create a positive body image and learn to effectively control your weight now and in your future? First you can learn to monitor your body composition as was discussed in Chapter 4. Then, you can use the following tips about eating disorders and body image to guide you. Once you review the tips, evaluate how you might need to change your perceptions about your body image now and in the future, and record your results in your cheer journal.

Body Image Factor

- *Genetics*—factors involving your heredity, which collectively have a major influence on how tall you are and how much you weigh as you develop in life. In the teen years, you are obviously growing quickly at different times, and your weight can change very rapidly. Accordingly, it is very important for you to develop positive eating behaviors, based on the recommendations at www.mypyramid.gov, so that you can control what you consume and learn to burn calories regularly to meet your energy needs.
- *Addictions*—abnormal signs of undereating, overeating, practicing dangerous behaviors like purging, and/or engaging excessively in MVPA.
- *Anorexia nervosa*—an eating disorder where an individual thinks she is overweight and stops eating enough calories to meet her daily needs. Find out more about anorexia nervosa at www.nutrition.gov by searching "eating disorders."
- *Bulimia nervosa*—an eating disorder where a person thinks she is overweight and then overeats, and subsequently forces herself to purge the food afterwards. Find out more about bulimia nervosa at www.nutrition.gov by searching "eating disorders."
- *Binge eating disorder*—an eating disorder where an individual often overeats due to feelings of guilt, depression, poor body image, or frustration. These individuals do not engage in purging. Find out more about binge eating disorder at www.nutrition.gov by searching "eating disorders."
- *Bigorexia*—a body-image disorder where an individual falsely believes that she is underweight or undersized.

#60: Cheer Nutrition and MVPA Myths

Objective: To help you learn about various cheer nutritional and MVPA myths

Equipment Needed: A pen and paper, a computer with an Internet connection, and your cheer journal

Description: With so much information about cheerleading, nutrition, and other types of physical activity available via the media, it is often difficult to determine fact from fiction. The following examples of cheer nutrition and MVPA myths are designed to challenge your current and future perceptions about proper cheer nutritional and MVPA behaviors. You can learn more about nutritional and MVPA myths by searching www.nutrition.gov and www.fitness.gov. Once you have reviewed the myths, evaluate how you might need to change your perceptions about what constitutes appropriate cheer nutrition behaviors, and record your results in your cheer journal.

Myth #1: It is reasonable to expect that you can lose 10-to-20 pounds in a week.

Reality: While someone might be able to lose this much weight in a week (although it's very, very unlikely), she cannot do so in a healthy way. Most of the weight lost this fast would be water weight loss, and the individual would become very dehydrated, weak, and unable to perform MVPA effectively.

Myth #2: It is best to eat only one or two meals per day to control your weight.

Reality: Teens need to eat several small meals per day to meet their energy needs, and to curb their hunger. Eating more often helps maintain your metabolism, keeps you energized, and helps keep you from overeating when you are very hungry.

Myth #3: It is easy to burn a pound of fat by just exercising.

Reality: To burn a pound of fat, you would need to expend at least 3500 calories, which is equivalent to a 135-pound person running non-stop for almost six hours at a 10-minute-per-mile pace. To lose a pound of fat weight safely in a week, it is best to reduce your level of food intake by 200-to-300 calories per day for the week and increase your MVPA by 200-to-300 calories per day for the week.

Myth #4: Foods like candy bars and sodas are best to consume at least 30 minutes before a cheer workout or competition.

Reality: Foods like these are high in simple sugars and can cause your blood sugar to rise quickly and then fall quickly, leaving you feeling tired when you need energy the most. Try eating fresh fruits or fruit juice instead if you feel that you need nourishment 30 minutes prior to a cheer workout or competition.

#61: Safe Cheer Weight-Control Strategies

Objective: To help you learn about safe cheer weight-control strategies

Equipment Needed: A pen and paper, a computer with an Internet connection, and your cheer journal

Description: You can learn to safely control your body weight by adhering to the recommendations listed below. The guidelines can help you avoid dangerous weight-control strategies, which are explained in more detail at www.nutrition.gov. Once you have reviewed the weight-control recommendations, design your own personalized weight-control program, and record your results in your cheer journal.

- Always check with your physician before you engage in a weight-loss or weight-gain program.
- Evaluate your BMI and waist circumference, as described in Chapter 3, and if both methods show that you are overweight or underweight, you may need to adjust your weight-control goals to gain or lose weight by working with a health/wellness professional or your coach.
- Use the dietary recommendations at www.mypyramid.gov and the MVPA recommendations at www.fitness.gov to guide you in designing a personalized cheer eating MVPA that meets your needs and interests.
- Workout regularly and work up to where you are maintaining a minimum of 225-to-300 minutes of MVPA weekly.
- Allow plenty of time for positive results (at least three months) as you are growing and developing.
- Keep a record in your cheer journal of your personal progress.
- Learn to recognize and avoid negative eating and MVPA behaviors, based on an inaccurate vision of what constitutes an appropriate body image.
- Reward yourself in positive and healthy ways when you achieve your goals.
- Regroup and adjust your goals, if necessary, if your initial goals become unachievable or too unrealistic.

6

Cheer Dance

#62: Get With the Cheer Music Beat

Objective: To learn and understand some basic music vocabulary, and how it relates to your cheer dancing

Equipment Needed: Music selected from a variety of styles (jazz, hip-hop, lyrical, march, etc.)

Description:
- *Beat*—A strong, repetitive sound that feels like a heartbeat. Clap your hands to the beat, snap your fingers to the beat, move your shoulders to the beat, move your hips side to side to the beat, bend your knees to the beat, step in place to the beat, and, finally, move around the space to the beat. Repeat to a variety of music selected.
- *Tempo*—speed. Repeat the previous drill to music that has a faster and/or slower speed. You should move exactly to the beat.
- *Measure*—Usually four beats. Walk four steps and change direction on the first count of each measure.
- *Phrase*—Music that sounds like a sentence. Most phrases consist of eight beats (two measures). Walk eight steps in one direction, and change your traveling movement (walk, run, skip, chasse, etc.) at the beginning of each new phrase to get the feeling of the phrase. Perform a selected movement sequence that requires eight beats to the music. The music phrase and movement phrase should begin and end at the same time.
- *Rhythmic patterns*—Similar to syllables of words. Words are divided into small parts, with some being short and some being long, such as pepperoni (pep-pe-ron-i, all short sounds) or pizza (piz-za, two longer sounds). Movements in this example might involve four jumps (pepperoni), and a straddle jump (pizza).

Reminders:
- Keep in mind that the beat holds the routine and all the cheerleaders together.
- Always listen for the beat and tempo of any music or cheers to be performed.
- Make each movement (syllable) very clear and distinct.
- Beats are like letters of the alphabet, measures are words, and phrases are sentences.

#63: Cheer-Dance Moves

Objective: To become knowledgeable about several of the basic dance moves that would be included in a dance routine

Equipment Needed: A notepad and pen (or computer) and your cheer journal

Description: It is important for you to understand the terms reviewed in this Tip in order to enhance your dance-movement skills in cheerleading. Read each term, and determine by taking notes in your cheer journal if you understand the term or if you need to learn more about the concept via the Internet or from coaches or parents.

Foot Movements

Ball dig: Place the ball of one foot next to the instep of the other foot.

Ball change: Shift the weight from the ball of one foot to the ball of the other. Used as a transition step.

Battement: An extended leg lift from the hip joint.

Chasse: Slide or step with the right foot to the side and have the left foot meet the right. Done on the ground or in the air.

Grapevine step: Step to the side with the right foot, step behind the right with the left, step to the side with the right foot, then step behind with the left (considered one grapevine step). Can be executed to the left.

Jazz square: Cross the right foot over the left, step straight back with the left, step out to the side of the left with the right—approximately 6-to-12 inches, and finish with the left foot beside the right. Can be repeated beginning with the right foot.

Locomotor movements: Walks, hops, jumps, slides, skips, runs—all of these can have variations such as large/small, high/low, fast/slow, and so forth.

Kick: A flicking motion from the knee joint with one leg.

Leaps/Jumps

Bells: Step on the right foot across the left, and push off the right foot into the air, bringing the left leg to meet the right in the air and clicking the heels. The knees are bent.

Cabriole: Same as bells, but both legs are extended straight.

Pike jump: Spring off the ground, with both legs extended forward and parallel to the ground; usually the hands reach to touch the toes.

Spirit/straddle jump: Push off from both feet, opening the legs into a wide second position (legs spread apart), but half the height of a toe touch.

Spread eagle: Push off both feet where the legs open to a straddle position, without using turn-out at the hips.

Jump splits: Push off both feet, splitting the legs in the air before landing in a split on the ground.

Stag (single): Brush the right leg from back to front into the air into a passé (hooked position), while keeping the back leg straight.

Stag (double): Same as a single, but the back leg is placed in an attitude (slight bend at the knee).

Trenches: Alternate doing a lunge position from right to left by sliding the toe of the working leg back and landing in a small lunge each time. The arms are usually swinging in opposition.

Tuck jump: Spring off the right foot, lifting the left leg into a passé (bent in front of the body), and at the height of the jump, raise the right leg to meet the left leg.

#64: Your Cheer Dance and Arm Movements

Objective: To learn how to make the arm movements during your cheer dance movements clean and precise

Equipment Needed: A mirror and a video recorder

Description: Common cheerleading arm movements are high-V, low-V, half-high and half-low Vs, diagonals, Ks, Ts, broken Ts, touchdowns, low touchdowns, tabletops, and punches. You should try to perform the motions in a sharp and precise way. Select three positions from those covered in Tip #63, and perform them in a specific sequence several times. Practice in front of a mirror to check for correct placement of the arms in space. Repeat with your eyes closed. This approach will help you feel and think about the muscles being used for each position. If possible, videotape the sequence of movements so that you can visually see if your arms are in the correct placement. Repeat by changing the sequences of arm movements. The movement sequence can be put to counts (like 5-6-7-8) to work for smooth transitions and a fast, precise, clean look.

Reminders:

- Use the muscles in the center of your the back more than your biceps/triceps.
- Do some type of exercise (push-ups, etc.) to increase your level of upper-body strength.
- Remember that weak upper-body strength can cause other body parts to misalign, which can raise your risk of being injured.
- Think of how the shoulder and elbow joint help in making clear arm lines.
- Apply tension to the arm movements as if you are pushing against something.

#65: Coordinating Your Cheer Dance and Arm Movements

Objective: To learn how to coordinate arm movements with dance steps

Equipment Needed: A dance-movement area that is safe

Description: Select one dance movement and one arm movement. Execute the two together. Keep adding a dance movement and arm movement into a short sequence, and repeat until you feel comfortable. Walk around the space, changing the arm movements every four counts, then every two counts, and then each count. Change the locomotor movement, and keep the arm-movement sequence. When comfortable with each of the sequences selected, continue to change either the dance movement or the arm movement. This exercise is something you can do anywhere, anytime. Keep repeating and working on the movement combinations that are difficult for you.

Reminders:
- Make sure you continue to have good body alignment (upright posture). Work on keeping your abdominals strong by performing sit-ups/crunches on a regular basis, which can enhance your ability to maintain the proper posture at all times.
- Perform repetition after repetition of your dance sequence until you don't have to think about coordinating your movements.

Dean Purcell/Getty Images

#66: Dancing to Enhance Cheer Core Stability and Coordination

Objective: To develop an awareness of core (center/abdominal) control of your body, especially when changing directions or positions

Equipment Needed: Music (you enjoy) with a definite beat (count) that you can follow

Description: Walk four direct, strong steps forward, and then walk four steps backward. Take a normal stride. Repeat with two steps forward and two steps backward. This exercise should be repeated with a variety of locomotor (running, skipping, sliding, etc.) movements and dance steps. In other words, once you can do the desired sequence with proper form while stepping, try running, then skipping, and so on, until you have improved. Advance to sideward directions after you have developed an awareness of the "core connection" when moving forward and backward.

Reminders:
- Keep your shoulders over your feet when traveling forward and backward. Do not lean your shoulders backward when going forward or backward.
- Feel the core/center connecting your upper torso to your lower body. Your upper torso should move back as your feet move backwards. If your upper body moves after your legs, your entire body is not moving efficiently.
- Remember that practicing and performing crunches/sit-ups can help develop a strong core.
- Use this exercise to assist you in making very clear, distinct body lines (improve your coordination and the flow from movement to movement), when cheering or dancing.

#67: Practicing Cheer-Dance Transitions

Objective: To learn how to make smooth, clear transitions from one movement to another

Equipment Needed: A safe, open space for movement (20-by-20 feet), and music (you enjoy) with a definite beat (count) that you can follow

Description: Select three movement skills. Randomly put them in order. Execute the three movements one right after the other, making the transitions smooth and clear with no hesitation (for example, a three-step turn around; kick one leg forward; turn on the balls of your feet, and repeat). Keep repeating the sequence until it flows together, and you have complete control of your body. Then, try putting the movements in a different order and practice them. Begin slowly, and when you feel comfortable with the transitions, gradually increase the tempo (speed). As a possible variation, change the direction or body level of the movements. For example, do a three-step turn on the balls of the feet, kick high, and turn to the side on ball change.

Reminders:
- Make sure to not hesitate between the movements executed. They should flow smoothly.
- Control your body movements, and focus on connection, alignment, and posture, while making the transitions.
- Focus on your "body control," so that you will be able to execute the movements at any speed, and will be able to move easily from one movement to another.
- Learn to gradually understand that the movements can be executed in different amounts of time (i.e., one count, two counts, four counts, etc.) or in half the time, such as "one and," or with two short movements, such as ball change.

#68: Evaluating Your Cheer-Dance Transitions

Objective: To evaluate whether you can move in a way that will make your cheer-dance movements more fluid (stronger), while using less energy and maintaining safety Equipment Needed: A mirror and/or a partner, a checklist, and a video camera

Description: Perform selected movement phrases (running, skipping, sliding, etc.) with a partner and/or for a video camera. Use the checklist for your partner or yourself to check the correctness of the movements demonstrated, adhering to the guidelines listed in this Tip. Enter your evaluation in your cheer journal.

Reminder:
- Focus on getting the most out of your movements, and try to make sure that your small muscles work as hard as your large ones.

Strengthen and Stretch (for all stretches, see Tip #38: Common Cheer Stretches)

Neck
- Make sure that there is no tension.
- Work to strengthen your neck muscles.
- Remember that forward leaning (causing your head to be out of body alignment) can cause aches and pains in other parts of your body.

Shoulders
- Keep them relaxed and pulled down.

Arms
- Use your back muscles to help hold your arms up and out. Don't depend entirely on the muscles of your upper arms (biceps/triceps).
- Be aware of your arm placement. Think about your balance and alignment, and control your core stability.

Rib Cage
- Breathe normally through your nose and mouth, and avoid belly breathing that can cause bad body alignment.

Pelvis
- Treat the pelvis like it is a bowl of water. Make sure it is upright so it doesn't spill out.
- Avoid arching your back backwards or pushing your hips too far forward.

Abdominals
- Develop strong abs to help keep your pelvis muscles under control.
- Use your abs to help you with the lifting of your legs.
- Remember that your abs connect the upper half of your body with the lower half (in addition, strong abs can help prevent chronic back pain).

Hip Joints
- Make sure that your hip joints are strong and flexible.
- Initiate nearly all leg movements from the hip joint.
- Develop turn-out positions from the hip, not from the knee.

Legs
- Make sure that the muscles that push outward (abductors) and the muscles that push your legs together (adductors) are both strong.
- Fully stretch your quads (front of thighs) and calves (back of lower leg).
- Stretch your hamstrings (back of your thighs).

Knees
- Avoid (locked out) hyperextended knees.
- Keep your knees over your toes when bending (plié) to help strengthen your adductors (inside of your thighs).
- Begin any elevated movement (moving up and down) with bent knees (plié) and end with bent knees (plié).
- Don't overstretch behind the knees, because it may lead to hyperextension (locked-out knees).

Feet
- Learn to use your foot joints. Landings from elevated movements should be toe, ball, and then heel, which can help absorb the shock of landing and may help prevent shin splints.

#69: Your Cheer Choreography

Objective: To understand the elements of choreographing a good dance routine for cheerleading

Equipment Needed: A CD player and two-to-three competitive cheer songs that your cheer coach uses in your workouts

Description: You can use many styles and methods to choreograph a dance. It is important to remember that choreography must have structure, such as writing a theme paper. The dance must have a definite beginning movement statement, such as a theme sentence. This "statement" should be a movement motif that will be repeated throughout the dance. It is the glue that holds the dance together, making it look complete. A movement theme or "motif" could be shaking your hands high in the air (two counts), shaking the arms low (two counts), shaking the hands out to the side (two counts), and kicking, with a toe-ball change (two counts). This eight-count movement phrase would be repeated several times throughout the dance. It could also be repeated with variations in direction and routines.

Think of writing paragraphs with your movement ideas. Select several dance movements that you want to include, and then figure out if they relate to each other, the music, and/or the idea of the dance. Each section/paragraph (four phrases of eight counts is usually a musical section) should focus on a different movement sequence that connects to the idea.

Decide where the climax or the most exciting movement phrase should be in the dance. It does not always have to be at the end, especially if it is difficult, such as a balance move. The ending needs to be strong and look easy for a lasting impression with the judges.

Every movement phrase needs to flow into the next. Walking from one formation to another breaks up the continuity of the dance. Create a variety of ways of moving/traveling from one formation to another or from one place to another.

Listen to the music carefully for phrases that sound alike. This step can help provide you with clues in choreographing and repeating movement phrases. Music is usually based on structures of verses and the melody.

Reminders:
• Structure and plan your choreography to look complete.

- Do not try too many different dance movements in one dance. The audience can only remember a short amount of movement at a time. If too much is happening, what will they remember? Repetition is important for emphasis.
- Invest time in learning about music and its structure, and you will better understand how it is put together. Dance choreography should follow the same structure as the music.
- Devote sufficient pre-planning and thought to your choreography. An outstanding dance cannot be choreographed overnight.

#70: Practicing Your Cheer Choreography

Objective: To practice the elements of choreography for cheerleading

Equipment Needed: An open, safe space with a smooth surface, and a CD/tape player with music that has a definite beat and rhythm

Description: Select three movement skills to combine together (for example, a three-step turn, kick, and ball of foot, and then change). Decide which to do first, second, and third (for example, ball change, kick, three-step turn), and figure out how to move smoothly from one movement to another. Perform to your music when confident with the sequencing. The sequence could be repeated continuously until it flows smoothly without any rests or breaks.

Variations:
- Combine the movements in different sequences.
- Change the direction of a movement or all movements (for example, facing front, execute a ball change while turning to the side; kick to the side; three-step turn sideward, but traveling to the front, while facing to the side).
- Add changes of body level to movements (for example, a ball change with a slight plié/bending of the knees, a kick, a three-step turn on the balls of the feet at a higher level).
- Add accents by making some of the movements very sharp/strong and the others flow.

Reminders:
- Utilize this drill to provide you with a moving foundation for future choreography.
- Keep in mind that the more you practice combinations of a variety of movements, the better you will be able to pick up movements and dance-step patterns quickly.
- Remember that all movement is initiated by a deep inspiration (lifting of your ribs), and your body control comes from a strong core/center/abdominals, especially when changing directions and levels.

#71: Practicing Your Cheer Full-Dance Routines

Objective: To understand what is required for an outstanding cheer-dance performance

Equipment Needed: A large, safe for movement space and a video recorder (preferred)

Description: Learn a dance routine from a friend or a video, or make up your own. Listen and watch carefully for all the little details of the movements. Before you begin rehearsing the routine, have an adult, a cheerleader, or a dance colleague watch your performance to see if you are doing each movement correctly. You could even videotape your performance, which would enable you to watch yourself to identify any mistakes. Once you have corrected the mistakes, you should rehearse the routine over and over until you do not have to think about what comes next. Continue to have someone (preferably different people over time) observe your performance and/or continue to watch videotapes of yourself for improvement.

Reminders:
- Clean up and perfect each movement when learning movement patterns, because the repetition of incorrect movement or errors can become learned behaviors, making them difficult to change.
- Regularly rehearse doing the routine full-out each time, since the body must learn movement patterns (muscle memory).
- Remember that you really are "performing" when you are able to perform the dance without thinking about what comes next.
- Perform the dance with more energy than you think is needed with all movements extended, clear, and performed to their fullest. A dancer must acknowledge the audience with confidence and a very direct focus.
- Include accents, gestures, stylization, and expressive qualities in your finished performance.

7

Cheer Tumbling, Gymnastics, and Movement

Grant Halverson/Getty Images

#72: Body Awareness—Cheer Swivel Hips (Half Twist)

Objective: To help build your body awareness and to assist you in learning new tumbling tricks, and perfecting old ones

Equipment Needed: A trampoline with spotters and a safety harness (preferred)

Description: Bounce on the trampoline three times, and then perform a seat drop (bouncing on your backside in a pike position, sitting up). Before you land on the trampoline again, straighten your body so you are perpendicular to the trampoline, with your hands above your head and your body turned 180 degrees. After you turn (but before you land on the trampoline), get back into the seated position and land in the seat-drop position again. Once you learn to do one swivel hips, try to do several in a row, or try to twist the opposite direction.

#73: Body Awareness—Cheer Seat Drop/Log Roll

Objective: To help build body awareness, with particular attention to introducing twisting movements into tumbling skills

Equipment Needed: A trampoline with spotters and a safety harness (preferred)

Description: Bounce on the trampoline three times, and then perform a seat drop. After you come off the trampoline from the seat drop, lay your body down (parallel with the trampoline surface), and twist one full rotation, using your arms to initiate the rotation. After you have completed the rotation, sit up into the pike position, and land on the trampoline in a seat drop. This maneuver is called the seat-drop, log roll. Once you learn to do one, try to do several in a row. If you want to get really fancy, alternate swivel hips with seat-drop log rolls, or try to do your log roll in the opposite direction.

Reminder:
- Learn to twist in the direction that you naturally tumble. For example, whichever hand touches the ground first when you perform a round-off is the shoulder you should turn over when you learn to twist. Practice this drill only after you perfect the swivel hips.

#74: Body Awareness—Cheer Swivel Hips (One and a Half Twists)

Objective: To help build body awareness, with particular attention to learning tricks that require multiple twists

Equipment Needed: A trampoline with spotters and a safety harness (preferred)

Description: Bounce on the trampoline three times, and land in a seat drop. When you come off the trampoline bed, get your body perpendicular with the trampoline bed, put your hands above your head, and perform one-and-a-half twists. After your twist is completed, return to a pike position, and land on the trampoline in the seat-drop position.

Reminder:

- Don't worry about the actual tumbling tricks you are learning. Follow the body-awareness progression of skills, and remember that it is okay to advance your body-awareness training before you are actually performing the tumbling tricks that the drills are designed to help.

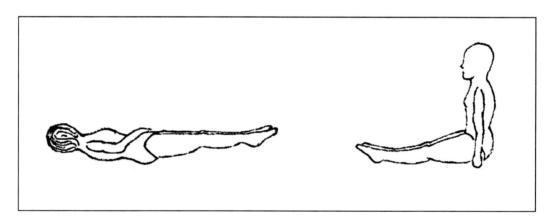

#75: Competition Preparation—Cheer Tumbling

Objective: To develop your level of mental and physical stamina that you will need for your tumbling movements in your cheer routines

Equipment Needed: A tumbling surface that you will use in your routine, or another safe tumbling surface

Description: Perform each tumbling skill that you perform in your routine by doing one skill after the other. Allow yourself a set amount of rest between skills, and reduce that rest period as you become more conditioned. If you start with 30 seconds of rest between tumbling passes, a possible goal for you might be to reduce that rest period to five seconds between the skills over a period of two months.

Reminder:
- Remember that tumbling can become extremely dangerous when you are fatigued. Do not reduce your rest period between skills too rapidly or you will increase the likelihood of suffering an accident. It is also important to strive for perfection with each pass. Remember: practice makes permanent; perfect practice makes perfect.

#76: Visualizing Cheer Tumbling Skills

Objective: To learn to train your mind to perfect your body's performance of tumbling skills

Equipment Needed: None

Description: Lay flat on your back with your eyes closed. See yourself performing each tumbling trick that you are working on in three different ways. See the trick in slow motion, as if you are a third person watching you practice. See the trick in regular speed, as if you are a third person watching you practice. See the trick through your own eyes as you are performing the trick. Always try to visualize perfection—see the trick perfectly done every time. Visualize each trick you plan on performing five times before each practice, just before you warm up. Visualize the tricks you are working on—plus the tricks you will be working on in the near future—10 times each every morning when you wake up, and another 10 times every evening before you fall asleep.

Reminder:
• Make sure you are relaxed before you visualize, and do your best to maintain total focus on the skills you are visualizing.

#77: Cheer Tumbling—Practice at Home

Objective: To increase your cheer practice frequency without overtraining

Equipment Needed: Varies from a safe, flat grass surface to a single 1³/₈ inch carpet-bonded foam mat (cheer strip)

Description: Once you learn and can safely perform a skill with no spotter, practice that skill. Most cheerleaders practice two-to-three hours each week. Most successful cheerleaders practice 12-to-15 hours each week. Cheerleading is a very practice-intensive sport, and paying a gym in which to practice every day may be cost-prohibitive. If so, buy a mat, or use your lawn (or a local sports field) to work on skills with which you are comfortable. If you need to practice a flip flop for 12 hours to perfect it (after you can safely do the trick with no spotter), would you rather use 12 weeks of tumbling class to practice, or 12 days after school? Save gym time for learning, and get your repetition practice on your own time.

Reminder:

- Don't forget to rest. If you're in a tumbling class, depending upon how many people are taking the class with you, more than half of your time will be spent watching. Learn to rest, while focusing on the matters at hand.

#78: Cheer Conditioning—Stomach (Abdominals)

Objective: To build the explosive power of your abdominal muscles, and to increase the stabilization muscles in your shoulders, chest, and upper back

Equipment Needed: A bar to hang from by your hands

Description: Hang from the bar, with your arms straight or slightly bent, and your body extended. Pull your knees to your chest, as shown in the illustration. Do this motion quickly, and then lower your knees in a controlled motion back to the hanging position, with your legs straight—without swinging—and repeat. This exercise is sports-specific, referring to the fact that you are duplicating a motion you use in tumbling in an exercise environment.

Reminder:

• Do not use crunches and other similar exercises in an attempt to strengthen your abdominals explosively. You use your abdominal muscles while tumbling in a certain range of motion, and you use them in a very explosive manner. To build explosive power, perform explosive exercises. If you cannot perform even one repetition of this advanced movement, bring your legs as high as you can in sets of 5-to-10 repetitions, until you build the strength to perform the exercise in its entire range of motion.

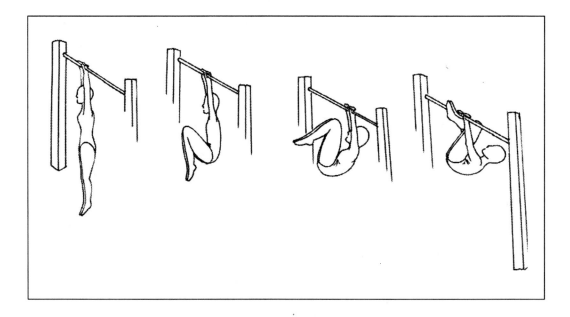

#79: Cheer Conditioning—Shoulders (Deltoids)

Objective: To build explosive power in your shoulders and arms, and to increase the stabilization muscles in your entire torso

Equipment Needed: A strong, durable wall structure that is tall enough to perform a handstand when leaning against it. Before doing this exercise, make sure that you will not damage the wall.

Description:

- **Handstand Push-Ups**—Perform a handstand against a wall so you are facing away from the wall when you are upside-down. Extend one leg completely, and bend the other leg, placing your foot against the wall (to help with balance). Start the motion by shrugging your shoulders, which completely extends your torso. Then, lower your body in a controlled motion until your head is half an inch from the floor. Push up to the extended shoulder-shrug position as fast as you can. Repeat.

Reminder:

- If you cannot complete one entire movement of this advanced exercise, start with a partial movement. Don't lower yourself all the way down. Lower yourself until you feel comfortable, and then explode upward.

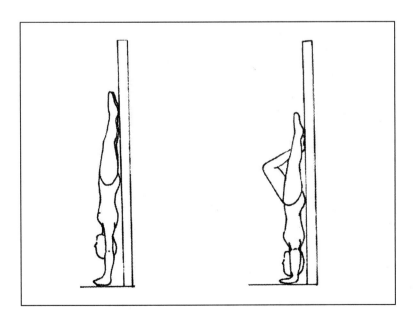

#80: Cheer Conditioning: Thighs (Quadriceps, Hamstrings, Gluteus) and Lower Legs (Gastrocnemius, Soleus)

Objective: To increase the explosive power of your leg muscles

Equipment Needed: A flat surface and box, or other elevated surface onto which it is safe to jump. The box should be 24-to-48 inches high, depending on your strength and ability level (for example, beginners would use shorter boxes).

Description: Jump from the ground up onto the box, and then stop. Then, jump backwards down to the ground and immediately jump back onto the box without hesitation. Repeat. The box should be high enough for you to be exhausted after 12-to-15 repetitions.

Reminder:

• If you do not have access to a box high enough to exhaust you after 15 repetitions, try to jump onto the box in a manner that allows you to land on legs that are more straight than bent. Do not land with your legs completely straight. All factors considered, the straighter your legs are when you land, the higher you had to jump to attain that position.

#81: Conditioning—Workout Planning

Objective: To help you learn to develop a sample workout plan

Equipment Needed: Varies, based on the type of exercises you do. See Tips #40 and #41 for more information.

Description: Plan your strength-building workouts in four- to six-week segments. You should be performing these workouts after you tumble, or, better yet, in completely different sessions. Keep these workouts under 45 minutes in length to keep your intensity level high, and perform the workouts three-to-five times each week.

Many different exercises can be performed for each muscle group, far more than those discussed in this section. If you have access to a weightlifting facility, get advice on proper training from a qualified professional and follow it. If you will be performing these workouts in your tumbling gym or at home, include plyometric exercises (bounding exercises that use your own body weight as resistance). Try to choose two exercises for each of your major muscle groups, and perform three-to-five sets of 12- to-15 repetitions per exercise. The main muscle groups with which you should be concerned are:

- Shoulder area (including arms)
- Back area (upper and lower)
- Abdominals
- Upper legs*
- Lower legs*

*Note: The muscles of your upper and lower legs will be worked together if you are performing plyometric exercises.

#82: Cheer Conditioning—Cycle Your Season

Objective: To help you learn and practice your cheer progression and training

Equipment Needed: None

Description: Failing to plan is planning to fail. Try to avoid the trap of doing what you have time for, or making up some exercises when you feel like exercising. Plan your year in advance, but be willing to adjust your plans as needed. If you start learning your training routine in August, and compete October through February, then you need to plan your conditioning workouts accordingly. In this instance, your off-season would be from March through July, while your in-season would extend from August through February. Accordingly, you should schedule your strength-building workouts much more aggressively (more often, with more difficult exercises) during your off-season. You do not want to stop strength training during the in-season portion of your year, but you do want to cut back a bit. If you are engaging in strength-training workouts five times per week for 30 minutes per session during the off-season, then you would taper that back to three times per week for 20 minutes during your in-season. You should follow a similar format with skill training. You should be learning as aggressively as possible during the off-season, and spending the in-season perfecting your skills and focusing on your routine. Cheerleading is a year-round sport, and you would be foolish to take extended vacations from your skill or strength training if your goal is to maximize your cheer potential.

#83: Improving Your Cheer Balance

Objective: To improve your balance, and concurrently, to enhance the strength of the small muscles surrounding your ankles—an effective way to reduce your risk of ankle injuries

Equipment Needed: A sturdy piece of board, large enough to fit both feet on at one time, and a half sphere made of wood, hard plastic, or metal. Affix the sphere, round side away from the board to the center of the surface.

Description: Stand on the board, which is balancing on the sphere, without letting the edges of the board contact the floor. Set a goal for the amount of time that you want to balance on the board. For example, when you start practicing, set a goal of 30 seconds. Whether you can balance without the board touching the floor for 30 consecutive seconds, or can only balance for two seconds at a time (repeated 15 times), keep up the effort until you reach your cumulative goal.

Reminder:
• When you need more of a challenge, try to balance on one foot, or balance on two feet with your eyes closed.

#84: Cheer Stunting Balance for Flyers

Objective: To increase your ability to maintain effortless balance in your stunt positions

Equipment Needed: None

Description: With your eyes closed, stand in the exact position that you would be in any given stunt. The goal in this instance is to maintain perfect balance, using only your ankle muscles, and without shifting your body weight or changing the position of your body. Set a cumulative time goal, and stick with that time goal until the exercise seems effortless, and then increase your goal.

Reminder:

• Start with the easier stunts, and progress to harder stunts as you get better. If you get really good, try changing from one stunt position to the next. If you have trouble with this maneuver, practice with your eyes open, and as you become more comfortable, start to close your eyes for brief periods of time.

#85: Conditioning for Cheer Competition

Objective: To improve your anaerobic (short, quick-burst activity) conditioning level to allow improved performance on the competition floor

Equipment Needed: A safe, open place to run (about 100 yards) and a stopwatch

Description: Warm up and stretch properly as you would before any rigorous activity, and then set your stopwatch or timer for 90 seconds. Take off running as fast as you can with no attempt to pace yourself. Continue this "sprint" until your timer sounds. When your timer sounds, continue walking for two minutes, and then sprint again for 90 seconds. If you are performing the suggested maneuver correctly, you will find that you are able to run much faster when you start than when you finish, which is acceptable, and normal. As the difference between your beginning running speed and your ending running speed narrows, increase the amount of time that you are running. A good guideline is to increase the time in 10-second intervals. Over time, you should increase the amount of time you are running until you are running for 30 seconds longer than your cheer routine lasts. This exercise is a great way to teach your body to function at the high level you will need during a routine, even when it is tired and running low on oxygen (anaerobic).

Reminder:

• Do not try to pace yourself. Learning to pace yourself is important if you are a runner, but you are using running as a way to train for a specific cheerleading activity. Pacing yourself decreases the effectiveness of this drill.

#86: Visualizing Cheer Competition-Day Routine

Objective: To create an environment that your body is familiar with to increase your comfort level at competition

Equipment Needed: None

Description: You should prepare the same way before every practice. Use the same visualization, same warm-up, same stretching, same drills, and same practice format. Doing so helps your body become accustomed to a routine that sets the stage for a great performance. You should repeat this preparation process on competition day. The underlying concept is that your body is comfortable with the preparation process that you go through on practice days, so you want to duplicate that process on competition day. This approach can help you be more comfortable and perform better when you compete.

At many competitions, you will have mat time only in certain increments, which may throw off your routine. In this situation, try to find out exactly how the warm-up process takes place at the competition you will go to next and develop a game plan. Know how you will warm up, and find a way to incorporate your preparation process from normal practices into the competition environment. You should also make it a point to actually practice the exact pre-competition routine that you plan on using for competition day.

Reminder:
- Remember that any way you can reduce your level of stress and eliminate surprises on competition day will help you focus on your performance.

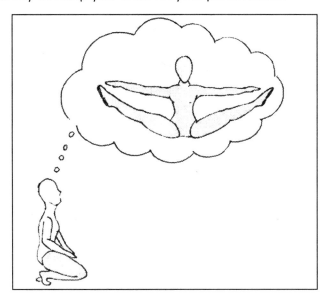

#87: Cheer Jump—Pole Drill

Objective: To learn proper torso and hip positioning for a variety of cheer jumps

Equipment Needed: A vertical pole or a post sturdy enough to support your body weight without the post shaking

Description: Grab the pole with both hands slightly higher than your head. Squat and jump off the ground, using your arms to increase the height of your jump, and to increase the amount of time that you are in the air. Your arms should begin slightly bent, and straighten as your jump takes you higher off the ground. As you reach the highest point of your jump, perform the cheer jump that you are practicing. The pole in front of you should help you keep your chest up in the correct position, and the increased time off the ground should allow you to concentrate on rolling your hips forward into the correct position. Snap your legs up and back down so your legs come together before you land. Remember that you won't be in the air this long without the pole. Only use this exercise to help you with jumps that do not require your legs to go directly in front of you.

Reminder:
• The pole drill is better than having a teammate or coach grab your waist from behind for one huge reason. The number-one problem that cheerleaders have with jump technique is the position of their chest. Your chest should remain perpendicular with the ground in most cases, and having assistance from behind encourages the jumper to lean forward with their chest.

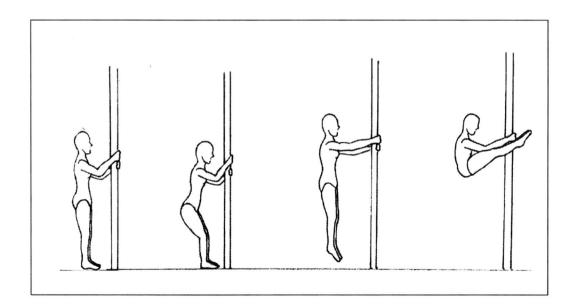

#88: Cheer Jump—High Kicks

Objective: To improve hip positioning during jumps, to increase flexibility directly related to jumps, and to develop strength in the muscles required to raise and lower the legs quickly

Equipment Needed: None

Description: Stand on your left foot, with your right foot just off the ground. If you need to, place a hand on something to help with balance. Without moving your right foot backward at all, point the right toe and kick the right leg as high as possible, while bringing your arms (or free arm, if you are balancing with something) into the T-motion. After your leg has reached its peak height, snap your leg back down as quickly as possible. Do not allow your right leg to go behind your left leg. As soon as your leg stops, repeat. Kick several times with one leg (a pre-planned number of kicks as part of your carefully-scheduled workout) before switching to your other leg.

Keep your chest perpendicular with the ground, and notice how your hips should automatically roll forward. When your hips roll forward, it increases your functional flexibility for the jump. In other words, it slightly tightens your lumbar (lower-back) muscles, and gives you some slack in your hamstrings (muscles in the back of your leg). Starting with slack in your hamstrings allows your leg to move higher before your normal range of motion limits the movement of your leg.

Reminder:
- This drill should be done in a very specific way to make it a helpful drill for jumps. When you start, you must not use your body for momentum. Your body should stay still, and you should use only your leg muscles to accelerate your right leg for the kick. It is also of great importance to maintain control. If you allow your right leg to swing behind your left after each kick, you will be using momentum to your advantage, greatly decreasing the effectiveness of the exercise.

#89: Jump Circle—Cheer-Workout Game

Objective: To increase the leg strength and endurance that you will need in your cheer jumps, and to improve your skill-related memory (useful for routines), while you have fun in a competitive environment

Equipment Needed: A safe place to perform jumps, with two or more cheer friends

Description: You and one or more friends stand facing each other, far enough apart to jump without placing the person next to you in danger. The first person should perform a jump—e.g., a toe touch. The second person would then do a toe touch plus a hurdler. The jumps would need to be done as part of a jump series, not individually. The third person would then do a toe touch, a hurdler, and a pike. If three people were involved in the exercise, it would now be the first person's turn again. That individual would perform each of the first three jumps and add the fourth. Each person decides which jump to add, making it part of the jump sequence. Participants are eliminated if they forget the order, fail to complete a jump, stop between jumps, or fall below some set level of performance, as agreed to by the participants before the start of the exercise (don't get their legs high enough, use technique below their ability level, etc.).

Reminder:
- To make the game easier, allow a pause between jumps. To make the game harder, each participant can add two jumps each time it is her turn.

#90: Cheer Jump Conditioning

Objective: To improve your cheer strength and endurance, particularly as they relate to the ability to perform jumps

Equipment Needed: None

Description: Start in either a high V-motion or however your coach has taught you to begin a jump. Squat relatively slowly (controlled) until your buttocks are close to your feet, and then explode as quickly as possible into a good tuck jump. To properly execute a tuck jump, remember to maintain proper arm placement, with your chest up, your knees coming to your chest (not the other way around), and with your hips rotating forward. Land with your legs slightly bent, and immediately begin the controlled, relatively slow lowering of your body back into the bottom, close to your feet position. Again, explode into the jump. No need exists to pause at the bottom position.

Reminder:

- Make sure that you are not landing in the squatted position, but rather lower yourself in a controlled fashion into the squat. Landing in the squat position has the potential for placing unneeded stress on your joints, thereby exposing you to possible injury.

#91: Practicing Cheer Motions With a Mirror

Objective: To help make you aware of the position of your body during a motion sequence or cheer, and to facilitate (help) your eye contact with the audience

Equipment Needed: A mirror, preferably one in which you can see your entire body

Description: Perform motions individually or as part of some type of sequence in front of a mirror. Make sure that you are performing the sequence correctly, and that you are aware of the proper placement of each of the motions in the sequence. Go through the sequence one motion at a time, and make sure to look at your entire body posture. Create some consistency through the motion sequence. Once you are comfortable with each motion and your ability to perform it correctly (good motion placement and correct body posture), begin to perform the sequence in sets of two motions at a time. Become comfortable, and then group the sequence into three motions at a time. Follow this pattern until you are performing one half of the sequence at a given time, at which point you should begin performing the sequence in its entirety.

Reminder:
• Make sure that you are smiling or making facials. Whatever your coach wants you to do with your face should be done throughout the process. You will probably feel silly doing it, but practice makes permanent, and the way you practice these motions will likely be the way you perform them. If you practice with a frown, then you will perform with a frown, which is not much fun for anyone to watch.

#92: Choosing Your Cheer Gym

Objective: To help you develop a checklist you can use when choosing your cheer gym.

Equipment Needed: None

Description:
- **Facility Safety**—When considering facility safety, make sure to walk around the gym you are thinking of joining. For example, does the equipment look safe? Are the mats torn? Are the trampolines frayed? Is the ceiling high enough to safely use the trampolines and perform basket tosses? Are things scattered around on tumbling surfaces? Are the people in the gym using equipment in an orderly fashion? Employ your common sense. It is also important that someone at the gym who is certified in first aid and CPR is present at any time the gym is operating. Also, the gym should have a well-stocked first-aid kit that is easily accessible, and emergency phone numbers posted near the phone. If any of these are missing, move on. Safety should be first, last, and always.
- **Coaching Staff**—Assessing the coaching staff is tricky. You want coaches who are well qualified and who have been successful cheerleaders at a level higher than your present level and/or who have coached your level well in the past, who understand how to safely teach the skills in your class, and, most importantly, who care about what you are trying to learn. It is also very important that at least one of the coaches at the gym you are interviewing utilizes a teaching style that you will learn from and/or has learned to tumble in the way with which you are most comfortable. If you and your coach do not communicate well, get ready for problems.

Reminder:
- Don't be fooled. Just because a coach holds a safety certification does not necessarily mean she uses safe methods for teaching. Just because a coach used to be the best cheerleader in the world does not mean she understands how to motivate and teach you. Just because a coach appears to care about you when you first visit the gym does not mean she will continue to care. Don't be afraid to let your decision about a gym be one that is made over time. Should you pick a coach who teaches poorly, you will undoubtedly end up with bad habits. Bad habits are very time consuming to fix, and are usually undo-it-yourself projects.

#93: Case Study on Choosing a Cheer Gym

Objective: To understand that you should consider your practice-time flexibility at the cheer gym you select

Equipment Needed: None

Description: Learning to cheer is mostly a do-it-yourself project—about 10 percent instruction and 90 percent repetition. When you look at how much time you will get to use while in class, you are actually looking at a few different factors: instructor-to-student ratio (how many students per instructor), structure of the class, length of the class, availability and convenience of additional practice time, and class content. This Tip details two different scenarios. Shannon is looking at two different gyms, and the breakdown of their classes. Which one should she choose?

Gym #1
- The class meets one time per week.
- The class is one hour long.
- The class ratio is 1:6 (one instructor per six students).
- The class will be used for 30 minutes of running tumbling and 30 minutes of standing tumbling. Warm-up time is offered before the class (with some guidance on how to do so properly), and time is offered after the class to condition (a conditioning routine is posted). During both the running tumbling and standing tumbling portions of the class, stations are created so you can practice, while you are not receiving instruction directly from the coach.
- You are allowed to come to the gym for one extra hour each week to practice tumbling or perform drills without direct coaching.

Gym #2
- The class meets one time per week.
- The class is two hours long.
- The class ratio is 1:8.
- The first 15 minutes of the class is spent warming up and stretching. The last 15 minutes of the class is spent doing conditioning. The middle 90 minutes of the class is composed of 45 minutes for running tumbling and 45 minutes for standing tumbling. During class, your group of eight students works one at a time with the instructor, and everyone else stands in line.
- Open-gym time is offered for 90 minutes on Friday nights for you to practice without direct coaching.

Gym #1 is the better choice. With a 6:1 ratio in a 60-minute class, you will receive about 10 minutes of hands-on instruction with your instructor (60 minutes divided by six students). The class is set up so that the remaining 50 minutes of the class is spent practicing. Gym time is available for you to warm up and stretch (which you really don't need a coach to help with), and the best part, Gym #1 makes time for you to practice whenever you want during the week. This package gives you a total of 110 minutes of practice time and 10 minutes of instruction, or about 92 percent practice and eight percent instruction, which is very close to the exact ratio you are seeking.

Gym #2 looks great through binoculars, but when you look closely, it's not that great. With an 8:1 ratio in a 90-minute class (you have to subtract the stretching and conditioning time because you can do this by yourself), you will receive about 11 minutes of instruction time. Unfortunately, you will not get much practicing done during class time, because this gym does not have drills set up for you to do, while the other people are being spotted. Also, this gym only offers extra practice time on Friday night—a night on which you're usually busy doing other things. In other words, this gym is offering only 11 minutes of instruction and an average of 22 minutes of practice time each week, which is not enough practice time per minute of instruction.

Reminder:
• Remember that when you are calling around to different gyms to start your process, Gym #2 would sound much better than Gym #1—two hours of class time and one and a half hours of open-gym time compared to one hour of class time and one hour of open-gym time. Picking a gym based on a phone call is like judging a book by its cover. Take the time to thoroughly look at the program you plan on calling home for the next several years.

#94: Choosing Your Cheer Gym Based on the Quality of the Facility

Objective: To help you understand the details of a quality cheer gym facility

Equipment Needed: None

Description:

- **Quality of Facility**—What type of equipment does your prospective gym have? Learning to tumble is possible with no equipment at all, but having different tumbling surfaces to learn on can make the potentially frustrating process much safer and easier. Accordingly, you should look for a gym that has a minimum of two floor surfaces to tumble on (cheer mat and spring floor); three surfaces would be even better (add a rod floor). These surfaces vary in resiliency (bounciness)—the rod floor being very bouncy, the spring floor being in the middle, and the cheer mat being fairly stiff.

  The gym you select should have at least one 7-by-14-foot trampoline. The material used for the bed will not matter for cheerleading. A tumble tramp is also a must. A tumble tramp is a type of trampoline that is a long (usually 30-to-60 feet long), narrow trampoline that is great for learning both standing and running tumbling. A gym's tumble tramp would ideally have an 8-by-16-foot crash mat at the end for landing, but an in-ground foam-block pit is okay, too. It is preferable that all of these trampolines be mounted flush with the floor of the gym (in-ground trampolines) in order to reduce the fear of falling off the trampoline while tumbling.

  Mirrors and conditioning equipment are also a must. For learning and perfecting dances and cheers, you need to be able to see yourself. Make sure your new gym has full-length mirrors covering a large enough area to facilitate easy viewing of yourself while you practice. During conditioning sessions, you will need more than just a floor. While you won't need to belong to a gym with a full set of weightlifting equipment, you will need, at a minimum, some bars to hang from and some boxes to jump on to perform plyometric exercises.

#95: Choosing Your Cheer Gym Based on Cost and Location

Objective: To help you understand the impact of cost and location to you and your family when choosing a cheer gym

Equipment Needed: None

Description:

• **Cost and Location**—When looking at a gym, cost is definitely something to consider. You can compare the prices between gyms in several ways. The first step is to take the cost for one year of tumbling and add it to all the registration or membership fees, required uniforms costs, and monthly tuition in a 12-month period, and compute a single "total" cost for the gym for a year. You can use this number, along with the number of classes offered and how that time is used in that same one-year period, to compare your gym options. The two example gyms from Tip #93: Case Study on Choosing a Cheer Gym can be used to refresh your memory and compare prices.

If Gym #1 has no registration fee, charges $50 per month, and holds classes 48 times each year (one hour per class, plus one hour of open practice time whenever you want, for a total of 96 hours per year), you would be paying a total of $600 (12 months x $50 per month) per year for classes. This translates into $6.25 per hour ($600 per year/96 hours) for time in the gym. Remember that each week at Gym #1, you receive 10 minutes of instruction and 110 minutes of practice, for a total of 5760 minutes per year (48 classes x 120 minutes). Accordingly, you would pay about $0.10 per minute ($600 per year/5760 minutes) for useable time either receiving instruction or practicing.

If Gym #2 has a $40 registration fee, and you have to spend $20 on a required uniform, classes cost $45 per month, and the gym holds classes 46 times each year (for two hours of class and 90 minutes of open practice time only on Friday nights), then you would be paying a total of $600 per year. This translates into $3.73 per hour of gym time. You also need to remember that you may only be available to use one Friday night of open practice each month, so adjust your numbers to $5.45 per hour of useable gym time—a little better than Gym #1. You also need to recall that at Gym #2, you will receive an average of 11 minutes of instruction time and 22 minutes of practice time each week. In other words, you would spend about $0.40 per minute of useable time either receiving instruction or practicing. As such, Gym #1 clearly gives you more bang for your buck (four times more bang).

The location of your new home is also something to consider. Choose a gym that is close enough to be convenient to attend frequently. Remember that cheerleading is a practice-intensive sport, so the more convenient the practice location, the more likely you are to practice, and the sooner you will reach your potential. Keep in mind, however, that buying rotten apples just because they are being sold close to your house is never better than driving to the good fruit stand to buy fresh, juicy ones—even if they do cost a bit more.

#96: Choosing Your Cheer Gym Based on Your Skill Level

Objective: To help you understand the importance of considering your skill level when choosing a cheer gym

Equipment Needed: None

Description: Some students excel in an environment where they are the best. They gain confidence—perhaps the most important component of learning cheerleading—by knowing that they are a role model for others. However, some students need to be constantly playing catch-up to remain motivated. Find out which type of performer you are, and use that information as a factor in choosing a gym where you will learn the fastest. You may be able to find both of these scenarios at the same gym on different nights of the week.

If you want to be on an all-star team, choose wisely. You do not necessarily want to be on the highest-level team you can find, because this team may not provide you with the best opportunity to become involved in the routine. If you join a team that is much higher than your current skill level, you will likely find yourself standing around, spotting, and hiding a lot—learning a few new skills and having very little fun. On the contrary, you also do not want to be on a team that is well below your skill level. Such a team would undoubtedly leave you unchallenged. You will probably be involved in everything in the routine, but none of the stunts will be hard for you, and all of the tumbling, jumps, and dances will be boring for you to practice. Either of these situations will likely leave you bored and discouraged by the year's end.

8

Competition Day

Doug Pensinger/Getty Images

#97: Visualizing Your Cheer Competition-Day Routine

Objective: To teach you to become mentally focused on the routine that you are about to perform

Equipment Needed: None

Description: Previously, the concept of visualization and its importance for learning new skills was discussed. It can be very helpful to be able to use those same techniques on game day. Before your routine, make sure your preparation routine includes visualization. Starting about two hours before your scheduled warm-up time, make sure you are physically ready to go (you are dressed, you have the music if it is your responsibility, your make-up and hair are done, etc.). Once you know you have everything ready for your competition, take some time before you warm up to see yourself being a champion. Visualize your routine from the second you set foot on the competition floor, through hitting each skill perfectly, to hearing your team's name announced, all the way to receiving your award. See this with counts of your routine first and with your routine music playing next. View the routine from the perspective of someone in the crowd and from your own eyes on the floor. Make sure to see everything perfect every time. Before you can show everyone else how good you are, you must see it yourself.

#98: Your Cheer Day Nutrition and Warm-Up Concerns

Objective: To develop a nutrition and MVPA plan for cheer competition days

Equipment Needed: A pen and paper, a computer, and your cheer journal

Description: On cheer competition days, you should plan ahead and prepare for your personal nutrition and MVPA warm-up needs. Use the recommendations detailed in this Tip to help you develop your own personal plan for your nutritional and warm-up needs on competition days. When you have reviewed the recommendations, develop and record your personal plan in your cheer journal so that you can refer to it in the future as a reminder.

Nutrition Needs

- Pack a sack lunch or snack with items that have a high percentage of carbohydrates, like bagels, fresh fruit, and pretzels.
- Bring a container that will keep fluids cool, and pack some fruit juice, low-fat yogurt, and/or a sport drink or two.
- Bring money for snacks or food to purchase and consume after your competition is completed for the day.
- Remember to pack enough, and if you share items with teammates, make sure you don't come up short on food and fluids for your own needs.

Warm-Up Needs

- Pack or wear warm-up clothing in case the area in which the competition is conducted is cold.
- Pay attention to the performance schedule, and allow at least 30 minutes for your individual and team warm-up activities (stretching, jogging, etc.) prior to your competition time.
- Relax between competition rounds (for example, between prelims and finals), and don't use up all your energy by running around. Enjoy socializing after your competitions are over.

#99: Cheer Competition-Day Checklist

Objective: To develop a checklist to ensure you are ready for cheer-competition days

Equipment Needed: Paper and a pen, a computer, or a printed list

Description: Make a list of everything you will need for the competition. Have your coach check your list a week before the competition day. When competition day arrives, go down your list and make sure you have everything you will need. If you are traveling in such a way that requires you to be apart from any of your luggage, make sure that everything you must have for the competition is in your carry-on, including underwear, socks, makeup, music (always have multiple copies stored in different places), your uniform, and shoes.

Competition-Day Checklist

- Cheer bag for equipment and supplies
- Hair bow
- Hair spray
- Hair brush
- Small mirror (if you do not have a place to check your outfit at the competition)
- Makeup (including glitter, if you use it)
- Shell
- Sports bra
- Sleeves
- Bloomers
- Skirt
- Socks
- Shoes
- Cheer warm-ups and jacket (if needed)
- Two copies of music (test each before you leave)
- Radio (unless your team has access to a community radio)
- Food (packed for before-competition routines) and money to buy food after the competition
- Headache medicine (with a parent's permission)
- Water and/or sport drink
- Any braces you may need
- Asthma inhaler (if needed)
- Athletic tape (if you need it)
- Chalk bag (if you use one)

#100: Cheer Team Relations and Personal Interaction

Objective: To become aware of positive teamwork and winning competitive-team behaviors

Equipment Needed: A pen and paper, a computer, and your cheer journal

Description: In cheerleading, like many other team sports or activities, you are competing as an individual, but you are also part of a team that gets scored in competition. By learning to be a good cheer-team member, you can become a better individual cheerleader, team member, and mentor to others with less competitive experience. Obviously, cheer competitions, like any other competitive experience (such as taking tests, reading out loud, giving a speech, etc.), create a lot of individual and team stress that can be expressed positively or negatively. The following information is designed to keep your competitive stressors positive. After you have reviewed the recommendations, develop and record your own thoughts about how you can be a better individual and team cheerleader on competition days in your cheer journal so that you can refer to them in the future as a reminder:

- Remember that it takes everyone on a team to be successful. Give your teammates words of encouragement.
- Act like you've been to major competitions before. Don't act too cocky if you do well, and be polite whether you win or lose. Congratulate your competition.
- Learn to tolerate others and their perceptions, because their perceptions will often be different than yours.
- Concentrate on the good things that happen to you and the team during competitions (and workouts, for that matter); focusing only on the negative things is non-productive, at best, and counter-productive in most instances.
- Learn to communicate your feelings in ways that are non-threatening to others.
- Learn and practice sharing by listening before speaking, and be accepting of other opinions.
- Lead by example, and be coachable.

#101: Evaluating Your Competitive Cheer Experiences

Objective: To learn to evaluate the positive and negative aspects of your competitive cheer experiences

Equipment Needed: A pen and paper, a computer, and your cheer journal

Description: In order to improve your competitive cheer performances and experiences, you should always take some time to reflect back (within a day or two of the competition) on what went right with your individual and team performance in competition. Obviously, your coaches, parents, and fans will have their opinions about what went right and wrong, but if you really want to become the best cheerleader you can, you need to be able to add or understand your perspective about your performance. By reviewing the following questions and developing your own reflection plan, you can begin to identify your individual and team weaknesses and strengths, and be in a position to be better able to maintain your strengths, while helping yourself and others to improve their weaknesses. When you have reviewed the questions, develop and record your own thoughts about your competitive cheer experiences in your cheer journal so that you can refer to them in the future as a reminder.

Competitive Cheer Experience Questions and Checklist

- Was I prepared well physically? Was the team prepared well physically?
- Was I prepared well mentally? Was the team prepared well mentally?
- Did I have fun? Overall, did the team do well, and did we get along well personally?
- Was I stressed out? Was the team stressed out?
- Did I have lots of energy? Was the team energetic?
- Was the coach happy? Was my family pleased? Were our fans positive?
- Am I still excited about cheerleading? Overall, does the team seem to be fired up?

Selected References

Fernandez, J.R., Redden, D.T., Petrobelli, A., and Allison, D.B. (2004). "Waist Circumference Percentiles in Nationally Representative Samples of African-American, European-American, and Mexican-American Children and Adolescents," *Journal of Pediatrics*, 145:439–444.

Headridge, P. (2005). *Cheerleading Chants* (videotape). Monterey, CA: Coaches Choice.

Headridge, P. (2005) *Pyramid Structure and Technique for Cheerleading* (videotape). Monterey, CA: Coaches Choice.

Headridge, P. (2005). *Transitional Cheerleading Stunts* (videotape) Monterey, CA: Coaches Choice.

Headridge, P. (2002). *Basic Jumping Techniques* (videotape) Monterey, CA: Coaches Choice.

Headridge, P. (2002). *Creating Excitement with Transitional Stunting* (videotape). Monterey, CA: Coaches Choice.

Headridge, P. (2002). *Fundamentals of Basic Stunting* (videotape). Monterey, CA: Coaches Choice.

Headridge, P. (2002) *Mastering Advanced Stunting* (videotape) Monterey, CA: Coaches Choice

Hutchinson, M.R. (1997). "Cheerleading Injuries: Patterns, Prevention, and Case Reports," *The Physician and Sportsmedicine*. 25 (9); 83–89.

Ivy, J. and Portman, R. (2004). *Nutrient Timing*. North Bergen, NJ: Basic Health.

Mueller, F.O., Cantu, R.C., and Van Camp, S.P. (1996). *Catastrophic Injuries in High School and College Sports*. Champaign, IL: Human Kinetics.

Mueller, F.O. and Cantu, R.C. (2004). *National Center for Catastrophic Sport Injury Research 22nd Annual Report, 2004* (www.unc.edu/depts/nccsi/AllSport.htm).

Rainey, R.L. and Murray, T.D. (1997). *Foundations of Personal Fitness, Any Body Can…Be Fit!* St. Paul, MN: West Publishing.

Rainey, D. L. and Murray, T.D. (2005). *Foundations of Personal Fitness*. Woodland Hills, CA: Glencoe/McGraw-Hill.

Strong, W.B., Malina, R.M., Blimkie, C.J.R., et al (2005). "Evidence-Based Physical Activity for School-Aged Youth," *Journal of Pediatrics*. 146: 732–777.

About the Authors

Tinker D. Murray, Ph.D., FACSM, is a professor of health, physical education, and recreation at Texas State University (formerly SWT) in San Marcos, Texas. He earned a bachelor's of science degree in physical education and biology from the University of Texas in 1973. He earned his master's of education degree in physical education from Southwest Texas State University in 1976, and completed his Ph.D. in physical education from Texas A&M University in 1984. His research interests include school-based and clinical-based youth physical-activity interventions for the prevention of obesity and diabetes, continuing education opportunities for coaching education, and personal fitness and training applications related to exercise physiology. Tinker is a fellow of the American College of Sports Medicine (ACSM) and a former two-time president of the Texas regional chapter of ACSM. He has worked since 1984 with his colleagues to conduct and publish research, and has written textbooks related to school physical education/athletic settings to promote physical activity in adolescents and college students. He is a co-author of a high school textbook, *Foundations of Personal Fitness*, which has been adopted by many school districts across the U.S. Tinker was a distance runner on partial scholarship at the University of Texas. He won the Texas relays marathon in 1977, and the Texas A&M marathon in 1978, 1979, and 1982. He had a best time of 2:28:30. He was also an assistant coach of cross-country and track at SWT from 1985 to 1987, and helped earn four championship titles in the Gulf Star Conference.

Mike Sardo has made a business of building and selling small businesses with the recurring theme of cheer industry specialization. He graduated *magna cum laude* from Texas State University (formerly Southwest Texas State University) in 1999 with a bachelor's degree in exercise and sports science and a minor in business. Mike was a four-year competitive cheerleader at Texas State University, and was elected as team captain for both his junior and senior years. He was ranked by the Universal Cheerleaders Association as one of the top 30 partner stunt performers in the nation for two consecutive years. While owning a gym in San Marcos, Texas, he provided training for the Texas State cheerleaders for several years. He was the Texas State

University head coach of the coed cheer squad and assistant coach for the all women's squad in 2003, which he coached to a UCA collegiate level national championship in the all women's division. He is presently a member of the collegiate style NBA professional cheerleading team, the San Antonio Spurs Coyote Crew.

Gladys M. Keeton, MFA, is an associate professor of dance at Texas Woman's University in Denton, Texas. She taught previously at Memphis State University and the University of Tennessee at Martin. Her undergraduate and graduate degrees were earned at Northwestern State University in Louisiana. She was director of the TWU modern dance group from 1969 to 1973, and the TWU repertory dance theatre company that toured Brazil in 1977. She is founder (1974), artistic director, and performer with the TWU international folk dance company that has performed at regional, state, and national conventions. Professor Keeton teaches modern, ballroom, tap, cultural dance, children's dance, and adapted dance with emphasis on pedagogy. She also teaches dance appreciation and choreographs for annual concerts and musicals, one of which received honorable mention from the Kennedy Center ACTF. Recognition includes the TWU Distinction in Service and Outstanding Academic Advisor awards, Outstanding Young Women of America award, the TAHPERD Outstanding University Dance Educator, honor, and PEPI awards, Southern District AAHPERD Outstanding University Dance Educator award, the Texas Drill Dance Team Educator's Association Hall of Fame award, and the Association for Retarded Citizens Outstanding Service award. Her contributions to dance education have been made through leadership positions in state, regional, and national organizations, as well as being selected as a charter member of the Texas Center for Educator Development in Fine Arts Cadre, Texas Education Agency fine arts advisory panel, state review panel for dance textbook adoption, the state board for educator certification dance standards review committee, and artist-in-education for the Texas Commission for the Arts. She is very active in the community as director of the TWU community dance center, directing special groups such as the Pure Emotion (special population) and Young at Heart tap dance company for senior adults, and conducting workshops for teachers and students.